Advance Praise for

How to Get Approved for the Best Mortgage Without Sticking a Fork in Your Eye™

"Don't waste your money
on Mortgages for Dummies!
It's completely outdated since
the Dodd-Frank Act.

*How To Get Approved
for the Best Mortgage Without
Sticking a Fork in Your Eye*™
empowers the reader to be an adept
and educated consumer ready to
make their American Dream
of home ownership come true
in today's mortgage world."

Thomas J. Haidon
NMLS #191229

"We are delighted to endorse Elysia Stobbe's book as well as her lending services! We were approved for truly the best possible mortgage. We remain loyal, 20-year members of two military credit unions (NFCU and Vystar). However, it truly pays to follow Elysia's tips and shop lenders using good faith estimates (GFEs). We avoided thousands of dollars in expenses by selecting a lender other than our military credit unions. Moreover, we thoroughly compared VA-loan options and because of the new world of mortgage financing and regulations, the VA loan was not our family's best choice."
~ *CDR James and Angela Peffley, USNR(Ret.) Melrose, FL*

"Take all or a piece of it…I just loved this book! I will definitely recommend that all of my clients read this book because an educated borrower gets the best experience and this book definitely provides all the education any buyer would need."
~ *Kristine Kennedy, Licensed Mortgage Originator*

"Elysia is knowledgeable and detailed as well as caring and compassionate. You know you are in good hands when working with her."
~ *Stephanie Proukou, Former Mortgage Originator*

What clients are saying about Elysia Stobbe.

"As a repeat customer I can say with enthusiasm that
Elysia Stobbe represents my needs first. I highly recommend
Elysia to help you with your mortgage needs."
~ Repeat Client, Mission Hills, MD

"Elysia is very personable and delightful. She took the intimidation
out of the loan application process, and never let more than
a few hours go by without responding to a call or email -
even while she was on vacation. The whole team is great!"
~ U.S. Military Veteran, First Time Home Buyer, Jacksonville, FL

"Elysia is a true professional. Elysia has so much knowledge
it is mind boggling! She treats me and my clients with
so much respect I referred my son to her!"
~ Realtor, Pikesville, MD

"I've known Elysia Stobbe for years and was thrilled to work
with her on our refinance. She works diligently for her clients."
~ Repeat Clients, Washington, DC

"I was a first time home-buyer and Elysia took all the time
I wanted to explain the lending process, again and again.
I couldn't have done it without Elysia!"
~ First Time Home Buyer, Jacksonville, FL

"I will highly recommend Elysia Stobbe to anyone and everyone that
I know that is buying a house. My experience with her and her team
was amazing. Everything went smooth and I felt as if they were all only
working on my file. The best experience I have ever had buying a house.
I will use her again."
~ Happy Home Owner, Jacksonville, FL

"Elysia Stobbe was fantastic to work with, always available
and was very patient. I would highly recommend her."
~ Relocation Client, Jacksonville, FL

"Elysia Stobbe and her team are simply the best. My wife and I built a house, and over the last year I have been working very closely with Elysia and her team. I can say with absolute certainly that if was any other company, and any other person my family would be in a different place then we are right now. I am eternally grateful to Elysia Stobbe for all of her hard work. If you need a loan or somebody in your corner to go to bat for you and get you the home of your dreams, then please call Elysia as she was instrumental in getting my family the home of our dreams."
~ Happy Homeowners, Ponte Vedra, FL

"Elysia always goes the extra mile, I trust her and recommend her to my family and friends."
~ Repeat Client, Washington, DC

"Elysia was very helpful every step of the way. She always made herself available by getting us quick responses to any question or concern. Additionally, she took the time to explain details about the process, which I appreciated considering I was not familiar with how to buy a home."
~ First Time Home Buyer, Jacksonville, FL

"Elysia worked with me on a very difficult refinance requiring multiple steps to complete. She obtained the refinance on our investment property that others said couldn't be done. She was extremely pleasant to work with and responded promptly to our many questions. She carefully guided us over all the hurdles and got the loan we hoped for! I gladly recommend her to anyone looking for a mortgage."
~ Experienced Real Estate Investor, Emerald Isle, NC

"During my recent mortgage application and closing process I had the great pleasure to work with Elysia Stobbe. Elysia exceeded any and all my expectations of what a Mortgage Professional would provide. Her level of professionalism, knowledge of the industry and individual attention to customer service puts her at the top of her profession. I will recommend her to anyone I know that is in the market for mortgage banking services."
~ Happy Home Owner, Jacksonville, FL

"Elysia Stobbe was recommended to me by several people I trust; her service exceeded my expectations. I had several dealings with so called mortgage professionals before, and working with Elysia is another level of service & integrity not found elsewhere."
~ *Client, Baltimore, MD*

"Elysia helped us with both of our homes, we recommend her to all our friends and family. No one will work harder for you."
~ *Repeat Clients, Palm Coast, FL*

"While there is always a lot of paperwork with home refi's, I was most pleased with the responsiveness and communication Elysia and [her] team provided. With their assistance I was able to skip two mortgage payments, get a lot of cash out, and therefore pay off a lot of bills. I highly recommend Elysia Stobbe and her team for your home loan needs."
~ *Retired Veteran, Home Owner with multiple properties, McLean, VA*

"Elysia has helped us purchase and refinance our home. We recommend her to all our friends and family. Elysia is a pleasure and professional."
~ *First Time Home Buyer, Palm Coast, FL*

"As a repeat customer, I can say with enthusiasm that Elysia Stobbe represents my needs first. She is professional and honest, and has always found the best deal for our particular situations. Our mortgage experience was professional with clear communication throughout; no surprises. I always recommend Elysia to everyone I know to help with their mortgage needs."
~ *Repeat Clients (together own 1 primary residence and 3 investment properties), Alexandria, VA*

"I couldn't have asked for a better person going to bat for me and my family. This was my first home purchase so it was completely over my head. Being a restaurant manager I know what great customer service is. She did not disappoint. Thanks again Elysia!"
~ *First Time Home Buyer, Jacksonville, FL*

"Elysia was able to make the challenging process of buying a home that much easier. She was able to immediately process our paperwork and alert us to our financial standings with our credit scores. Her level of responsiveness was beyond reproach as there was never an issue getting access to her or her support team. Elysia is on your side throughout the process, from start to finish. In addition to the levels of service she provided us with, Elysia was able to find us the best rate on the market, and enabled us to close within a 30 day period. There were no issues and the funds were available at closing without any problems. We were thrilled to have her in our corner and would highly recommend her to anyone ready to become a home owner."
~ Happy Home Owner, Neptune Beach, FL

"As first time home-buyers, Elysia helped us throughout the loan process, making sure important deadlines were met and that we understood each step of the process. Each time that I have contacted her, both before and after the closing of the loan, she has been responsive, professional and a pleasure to communicate with. Not only was she present at the closing, but she prepared a detailed booklet of important information and documents in advance so that we could review anything we may have questions on. Overall, Elysia was terrific and I would recommend her to anyone closing on a home."
- First Time Home Buyers, St. Johns, FL

"I want to thank you for all your extra work. At times this process has been trying and stressful, but I always felt better after talking with you. Thanks for all your patience and knowledge. Your positive attitude and sense of humor helped pull us through, to reach our dream."
- First Time Home Buyers, Jupiter, FL

"Elysia and her team made the mortgage approval process very easy. With my husband and I in different states, being able to send things electronically and sign electronically made everything so easy. They were on top of things, kept me informed and answered all my questions! It was all relatively painless. I've already recommended Elysia to a friend."
- Happy Home Owners, Apopka, FL

Elysia Stobbe

HOW TO GET APPROVED FOR
THE
BEST
MORTGAGE
WITHOUT STICKING A FORK IN YOUR EYE™

ELYSIA STOBBE

Ponto Alto PUBLISHING

Maria Stobbe NMLS #146751

Ponto Alto Publishing
1431 Riverplace Boulevard #1404
Jacksonville, FL 32207

First Ponto Alto Publishing softcover edition June 2015

For information about special discounts for bulk purchases, please contact Ponto Alto Publishing Special Sales at info@bestmortgagebook.com

To contact Elysia Stobbe about speaking at your live event, email info@bestmortgagebook.com

Back cover photo by my incredible friend and stellar photographer Beth Meckley
flickr.com/photos/bmeck16/

Manufactured in the United States of America

ISBN 978-0-9861620-0-8

ISBN (ebook) 978-0-9861620-1-5

"The ache for home lives in all of us. The safe place where we can go as we are and not be questioned."

~ Maya Angelou, *All God's Children Need Traveling Shoes*

Success comes from taking the initiative and following up...
persisting...eloquently expressing the depth of your love.
What simple action could you take today to produce
a new momentum toward success in your life?

~ Anthony Robbins

Acknowledgments

So many of my friends and colleagues have made this possible—I am grateful to be surrounded by so many giving, curious, loyal, and amazing souls. My brain is filled with immense respect for those who have taught me the ever-changing mortgage business. My heart is filled with joy and gratitude for the clients that have let me glimpse their personal lives while helping them navigate the tumultuous mortgage environment and help them achieve their dreams. It is a privilege to serve and help my friends and clients achieve the American dream of home ownership. Every day that I am able to help facilitate a client's wishes, it gives me happiness and fulfillment.

I am so thankful to the amazing friendships and brain trust that I am so fortunate to have in my life. Thank you to my friend Michael J. Frueh, Director, and Mark Connors, Lender Liaison at Loan Guaranty of the U.S. Department of Veterans Affairs, for spending time with me to help educate the outstanding veterans that let us live free. For their help and great feedback regarding real estate agents, I would like to thank Gary Keller, Co-founder and Chairman of the Board; Mark Willis, Member, Board of Directors; Jay Papasan, VP of Publishing; and, Patti Siebold, Broker, of Keller Williams International. Additionally, I would like to offer a super thank you to Patti for that unexpected very long ride across Austin during our seminar. Thank you to Dolly Lenz for insight about Realtor®-client relationships. Thank you to my early-morning friend Wally Conway for his wisdom regarding home inspections. Thank you David Miller, CEO, and, Daniel Miller, Associate Agent Owner, of Brightway Insurance for sharing your insights.

Thank you to my Mama, who always told me to "do what you enjoy and the rest will follow." Special, amazing thanks to my best friend Marisha Chilcott for being an outstanding human being and a supportive sounding board for me. Thanks to Lori Day, my first coach, for starting me on the path of coaching and growing. I am also grateful for my coaches Tanya Thomas, Patty Morehouse, and, Ted McGrath; and, for my wonderful friends at Tony Robbins Platinum Partners for their support. A million hugs to Tony Robbins for re-opening my heart. I am forever grateful!! Most important, special thanks to my editor, Lis Hylton, for being more than an editor. Lis has been creative, patient, and, supportive during my relentless mission to deliver this book to those who will become empowered by reading it. Lis, you inspire me and help me grow—thank you.

Contents

Introduction

Why have I written a book about mortgages? Because in my many years of helping people get into homes, I have found that there isn't a mortgage book available that helps to make the process more accessible to those that are not mortgage professionals. I feel that everyone interested in buying a home needs and deserves to know what's involved in the mortgage process. It's typically the largest single expense in a person's life, yet most people don't know much about the process, about what to expect, and how to prepare so that the process is focused on fulfilling a dream rather than confusion and stress.

Most people don't know how much home purchasing power they have, how much to expect for closing costs (varies by state), or how much paperwork is involved when applying for a home loan. Most people have no idea the difference between loan programs from bank to bank, lender to lender, or broker to broker — or what the differences are between the main types of residential mortgage providers. Most people have no criteria for choosing a lender, the type of loan to seek, or how much down payment is best for them. For example, are there differences between the types of property that may affect down payment?

The mortgage industry is packed with nuance, which can lead to confusion for the consumer. While trying to buy a home, you may have people from many different professions telling you what you should do and how to make decisions—who should you listen to in which situations? Your most personal financial information is critical to the mortgage process and yet do you know who you are sending it to? What about mortgage insurance? Why is it required and when?

The two questions I most often hear are: "What's the payment?" and, "What's the interest rate?" While these questions are important, there are several other questions that are just as critical: what is the right loan type for me; is there an up-front funding fee for this loan; what are the differences in available mortgage insurance; how will property type restrictions affect my loan; what are the pros and cons of this loan; what is the down payment requirement with this loan choice over another; what are the closing costs associated with each loan type; and, who is allowed to pay the closing costs? Successfully navigating the maze of questions, regulations, and requirements ultimately leads to a mortgage closing.

Through over ten years of experience, thousands of clients, hundreds of Realtor and builder transactions (time line constraint purchases), and, as a licensed loan originator in 9 states and the District of Columbia, I have developed a wealth of knowledge about regulations and requirements. My commitment to client service and caring about their home buying experience has driven my passion for the individual personal experience in the mortgage industry and how the regulations and requirements affect real people in real time. With this book I'm privileged and excited to share my knowledge and experience with you. After reading this book, you will have an understanding of the big corporations that loan money to home-buyers, what other options you have and how to navigate government regulations and requirements to your advantage.

I feel that an educated consumer is my best customer and I am happy to share these mortgage tools and tips with you in the hopes that you educate yourself and find the best mortgage and the mortgage professional that is right for you. In addition, I want you to know what to expect, what to ask, and, who to ask to get the answers you want and to understand what those answers really mean. With each chapter I will guide you through the mortgage process, from choosing between different loan types, to understanding the difference between a Good Faith Estimate and an Itemized Fee Worksheet, to the necessity of submitting certain documents in a particular method, and finally how to enter Closing Day stress-free and knowing that you have gotten the mortgage that makes the most financial sense for your future. The goal is to help you get the best mortgage possible for your individual needs and get to closing on time, stress free!

This book is for informational purposes. It is not intended to provide income tax advice, financial advice, or, credit counseling. It is not intended to approve or deny a mortgage application—it is a guide to help you have a clear understanding of the sometimes-cryptic mortgage market. The mortgage lending and credit environment are always changing. For the best and most current information ask your trusted licensed loan officer. In the meantime, here is everything you need to know about mortgages, that no one will take the time to explain to you. Enjoy!

①

How Can You Apply This Book to Your Advantage?

The best way to use this book is to read what interests you first and then start at the beginning and read it to the end. I set up this book to be the most useful road map through the steps in the mortgage loan process. I've arranged the chapters in a particular order; this order represents the sequence of becoming informed and taking actionable steps to obtaining the best mortgage when purchasing a home. If you are currently interested in refinancing, you've already been through some of these steps.

For those of you that are about to embark on the journey of purchasing a home with a mortgage, the sequence of chapters and actionable steps in the process, may be different from what you have imagined. The next three chapters will provide you with a broad understanding of what is involved in getting a mortgage. Chapter 2 explains the difference between pre-qualification and pre-approval. The advice in Chapter 2 is intended to help you understand why getting pre-approved is the most stress-free way to shop for a home.

Chapters 3 and 4 will help you understand the ins and outs of the mortgage industry and the people working in that industry. This knowledge will help you choose the best lender and the best people

---

Make your new house a home — for less!
Visit ashleyfurniturehomestore.com to shop furniture and accessories, and find an Ashley Furniture HomeStore near you.

to include on your team. Without this information, how in the world does one make a sound choice? Every bank or mortgage company is going to want your business. These chapters will empower you to ask questions that will make these institutions and their staff answer questions beyond their phone scripts and advertising slogans.

Once you have a good understanding of the mortgage industry, Chapter 5 provides an outline of the 4 Keys to Qualifying for the Best Mortgage. In Chapter 5, I explain the 4 Keys and how they work together to get you the best mortgage: a mortgage you can really afford, a mortgage you understand. In Chapters 6 through 9, I explain each of the 4 Keys in great detail. These details will empower you to be an active voice during the loan application process; the details will provide you with the knowledge needed to be aware of each step in the process so that you can make sure each step is utilized and working to your advantage.

In Chapter 10, I explain the 4 Stages of the Mortgage Process— origination, processing, underwriting, and closing — all of the previous chapters are meant to prepare you for these four stages. What you have learned can make this process much easier and much less stressful than it is for those that go in just hoping someone is going to have their best interest in mind. I've been incredibly lucky to have started my career with and continue to work alongside processors and underwriters that are ethically committed to the client—but, but, but… I have heard the stories and examined the past transactions of people that unfortunately encountered individuals that have acted either with disregard or pure laziness when it comes to getting the best deal for the client. You have this book in your hands, so don't let that happen to you!

In Chapters 11 and 12, I'm going to walk you through the meat of the documents and fees that are going to come up in the 4 Stages of the Mortgage Process. Again, this information will empower you and enable you to understand what your mortgage professionals are talking about and why they are talking about it. And, to ask them if they aren't talking about these important things!

Chapters 13 and 15 cover mortgage Loan Programs and the Loan Terms that will go along with the program you choose. Why are these chapters after all of the rest if I'm telling you to let things happen in this order? You definitely want to apply with your lender BEFORE deciding which loan program you are going to use. Your lender will tell you which programs you can qualify for and can answer questions about the different options available to you.

Chapter 14—thank you to all service members and veterans—this chapter is for you! The absolute best mortgages available are reserved for those that are currently or have in the past served in the United States armed forces, and the spouses of service members and veterans. I have a vast amount of experience working on VA loans and I have taken special care in this chapter to share my knowledge and experience with you. I consider it a privilege to help those who serve us. Not a day goes by that I don't look out my office window and know and appreciate that I am free because of our armed service men and women. There are many nuances that can be used to the advantage of the VA loan borrower. Not all lenders who can originate VA loans are empowered with the knowledge to get you the best VA loan. This chapter will open the door to those secrets.

Chapter 16 explains something that blindsides many home-buyers—insurance. Do you know how many people didn't know that if they put down just a few thousand more dollars they could have avoided tens of thousands of dollars in required mortgage insurance payments?

I've included the information in chapters 17 and 18 because I know choosing the right lender isn't the only confusing and overwhelming decision when it comes to deciding who to help you get the best home. These chapters provide you with pointers on choosing the best real estate agent and the best home inspector. And, these steps are much farther along in the process because I believe the process is much smoother if you get your loan pre-qualification or pre-approval before getting a real estate agent. If you get the real estate agent first and begin looking at homes as your first step in the home-buying process, you're putting the proverbial retired hen before the egg. Becoming informed about the mortgage process is the twinkle in the hen's eye; getting pre-qualified or pre-approved for your mortgage is the egg; searching for a home, getting an inspection, and writing a contract are the phases of the chicken's life.

Now that you have all of the best people working for you, Chapter 19 prepares you to make the best deal with the seller of the home you want. Once you execute a sales contract, you are committed and in a legally binding contract—that means you are expected to perform. If something goes wrong, you stand to lose a lot of money. This is why you want to do all of the mortgage work long before you ever choose a home, and this is why you also want the best real estate agent and the best home inspector. Avoid the mistakes and tragedies of those that forgot to get informed before setting out to get a mortgage and buy a home. Since YOU have avoided those mistakes, you are on your way to closing day in Chapter 20!

Chapter 21 explains government involvement in the mortgage industry. Many of the things that seem really annoying are actually required by the government, and, most of these things are in place to protect you.

Finally, I've dedicated Chapter 22 to those of you that feel a mortgage may be out of reach at this point, but want to be informed now and start taking steps towards qualifying for a mortgage in the future. Whether you are still in college and wanting to get ahead of the game to make the right choices now that will help you later, or, if you have recent bad credit and want to form a plan to inspire you towards regrouping and getting a mortgage later, I have some advice for you in this final chapter.

Throughout the book we've included interviews with industry experts to help you gain additional perspective from different viewpoints. We've found great partners to give you discounts and free stuff that will help you save money as a homeowner. I have also included some fun and not so fun stories to keep you from boredom. After all, mortgage paperwork is not the most exciting way to spend your afternoon. I get it, and I do everything I can to try to make the experience as painless as possible by providing you with the tools you need to get the best mortgage for you. We've added charts and paperwork examples to make it easy for you to find out what you need, must know, and must ask your lender and your real estate agent. The checklists are helpful to get you up and running. If you get stuck along the way, or have any questions just shoot me an email (info@bestmortgagebook.com) and my team and I will be happy to help you.

Again, thank you for reading my book. I hope you use this guide wisely and to your advantage.

②

Why Get Pre-Approved?

What's the Difference Between Pre-Qualification & Pre-Approval?

The differences between pre-qualification and pre-approval may seem minor, but they can be huge when it comes to actually closing on your dream home. Watch out! Not all lenders offer the more thorough pre-approval. If your lender only offers pre-qualification, or you choose to start with pre-qualification, make sure that you are as detailed as possible with the information that you supply. As you'll read in the rest of this chapter, I strongly recommend that you at minimum pre-qualify. Get pre-approved if it's an option!

Pre-qualification is the process of determining what you may qualify to purchase with a home loan. You will be required to give your name, address, income, assets, and, credit history to your lender. The lender will pull your credit and based on the information given determines what, if any, loan programs you qualify to use in purchasing your new home. It is very basic and leaves lots of room for misinterpretation on the part of both parties. The challenge is that you may give the lender your gross income before tax deductions, basic asset information and unknowingly leave out critical information that may be key to your loan qualification. This is concerning because you may end up home shopping in the wrong sales price range, or, worse, may not actually be able to close on your dream home.

Pre-approval is the thorough process of providing your name, address history, work history and income documents for the last two years, along with your asset statements. The lender is able to review the information and correctly calculate your income and debt-to-income ratio, and, review your funds available for down payment and reserves. It may not seem like a big difference, just more documents and a few more questions to answer. However, it can save you lots of disappointment and heartache during the loan process. It will also set you up for success when your loan process begins and help with processing your loan more quickly if your lender has the documents ahead of time. By providing the documents ahead of time, the lender can assess how your income will be calculated and make sure you can use the funds you have available. Once you supply documents for loan qualification, you will begin to see the differences in the way most borrowers look at their documents vs. the way lenders review the documents and underwrite to the loan requirements.

Pre-Qualifying & Pre-Approval Make Home Shopping Much Easier

You should get pre-qualified to find out what price range your dream house needs to be within according to your current financial budget. Pre-qualifying allows you to find out exactly how much money a lender is willing to give you based on your income, assets, and other data. Having a pre-qualification will also give you confidence to make an offer when you find the right home.

Finding out the exact dollar amount that you can get from a lender will allow you to focus on homes that you can buy, rather than waste time on homes that are well below or above your pre-qualification dollar number. What if you think you can buy a house for $400,000, but your lender says you only qualify for $250,000. That's a big problem if you did not pre-qualify before writing a sales contract, and, if you had your heart set on that specific property as your new home. If you write a sales contract that you are unable to follow through on, you could lose a lot of money.

You don't want a mortgage that is going to jeopardize your financial future because payments become overwhelming once you have moved into your home. Pre-qualifying can empower you and take the stress out of your home search— you'll know which homes to consider and which homes to avoid. You can search for your dream home knowing that you are qualified for a mortgage that you can afford. Remember the questions to ask yourself when choosing a lender? Make sure you have chosen a licensed loan officer that is motivated to get you the best possible pre-qualification based on as much information as possible. So, the three major reasons to get pre-qualified are to get all of the info on the table from the start, to prevent losing $1,000 or more because you paid fees and then found out you didn't qualify, and, to get a full assessment since your adjusted gross income is not equal to your salary— definitely a big surprise for many people. You don't want any of these three surprises!

The Less You Give the Lender, the More you Hurt Yourself

If you go in thinking you are going to tell your lender how much money you make and how much you would like to borrow, and they are just going to give it to you, applying for a mortgage is going to be a big shock for you. Although such simplicity would be wonderful, unfortunately this is not how it works. A mortgage loan is a privilege that is earned through the establishment of good credit, ability to repay, collateral, and, many other factors we'll talk about later. While it's true you can walk into a car dealership and get approved for a car loan in as fast as 10 minutes, getting a mortgage loan requires a lot more information and takes more time. The tedious part is supplying information to your lender and having that information verified. You can tell your lender whatever you want, but the more accurate you are and the more honest and forthcoming you are, the better and faster the process for getting your mortgage.

I have had people tell me all kinds of stories, good and bad. There is a small amount of consideration for extenuating circumstances, but the bottom line is always the numbers — your financial ability to repay the loan. When you pre-qualify, the lender is determining your financial ability to repay the loan based on a strict set of regulated guidelines. These guidelines include how much money you can show on paper (W2's, 1099's, Federal Tax Returns), how much money you have in the bank, and, how much debt you are already obligated to pay back. By being open, honest and up front from the start regarding your income and credit, working with your lender as a partner puts you in the best position to actually close your loan. That's your goal, right?

Don't Waste $1,000

But, before you close your loan, you need to find your dream home and write a sales contract on it. Once you have a fully executed sales contract (signed by all parties), you are off and running– and spending money. You will have time deadlines in your sales contract, such as home inspection, appraisal, loan application, loan approval, when your earnest money deposit (aka binder money) is up for grabs. These are real deadlines as you are in a written legal contract and expected to perform. If you do not perform, you can lose your earnest money deposit (aka binder, depending on what part of the country you are in). Not only is your money up for grabs, but you will also spend money to comply with the contract you have signed.

Your real estate agent and lender should discuss these deadlines with you so you know what is expected and so that you are all on the same page. But if they don't— remember, it is you who signed the contract and it is you who is ultimately responsible. Make sure to ask questions! Okay, so lets get back to the cold hard cash you will spend BEFORE you close on your new home. You should budget $750-$1000, depending on the amount of your loan and where you are located. The most expensive thing you will pay for out-of-pocket before closing is usually the appraisal.

An appraisal usually runs about $350-$550, depending on the type of appraisal. The type of appraisal can vary depending on whether you are buying a primary residence or an investment property. Sales price can also affect the cost of the appraisal. If you are buying in the Jumbo range and applying for a larger loan amount, over $417,000, the appraisal will cost more. If you are applying for a mortgage (as opposed to paying cash for your new home) you will pay for the appraisal, but the lender actually owns it. Yes, this is money you pay so the lender can evaluate your property. Although you pay for the appraisal, the lender owns it— you read it correctly the first time. Kinda crazy, huh? Well, that's the way it is. The good news is that you are entitled to a copy of it (usually per regulations you must be supplied a copy of your appraisal at least 3 days before closing, unless you have waived this right in writing).

More good news, the appraisal is for your protection as well as the lender's protection. The appraisal protects you from paying more than the home is actually worth, while also protecting the lender from loaning money on collateral (your new home) that's not worth the sales price. You will pay for the appraisal regardless of whether or not you actually are approved for the loan and/or buy your new home. Plus, don't you want to know that a professional has evaluated your property, comparable home sales, and that the home is worth what you are paying to buy it? Okay, thought so.

You will also pay for a home inspection. Again, this is for your protection. A home inspection will cost you around $250-$400 depending on what's included. Depending on the type of loan, the lender may or may not require a copy of your home and pest inspection. If you're wondering about the differences between an appraisal and a home inspection, you're in good company! I've explained the differences in Chapter 18, How to Choose a Home Inspector.

A home inspection may not be required. If that's the case, should you spend the money to have it inspected? YES! If you are not comfortable spending an average of $350 to find out if you will need to spend $7,500 on a new roof in the next 4 years, then you may not be ready to be a homeowner. This is where an ounce of prevention can prevent a pound of pain. Lots of pain. Home inspections can alert you to problems with the home such as mold, Chinese drywall, sub par wiring, leaky roofs, missing insulation, water damage, broken pipes, faulty electrical panels and much more.

Depending on the type of loan, you may also get a pest inspection. If you are getting a VA loan, a pest inspection is required and you are not allowed to pay for it; typically the seller will pay for it. Pest Inspections, aka WDO (wood destroying organisms) Report can let you know if there are wood destroying organisms such as termites, carpenter ants, etcetera present now, or if pests have been munching on your about-to-be-new home in the past and what damage has been done. Don't you want to know if you've got bugs (gross!) in your new house before you decide to buy it? Some inspectors are qualified to do both a home inspection and a pest inspection, so some will give you a combo deal. Choose a licensed home inspector wisely. I hear horror stories of home inspectors that also have construction companies and use the inspections to funnel business to themselves. This is NOT always the case, but buyer beware.

To sum it up, getting pre-approved with a good lender that has a great success-closing ratio (see our checklist at the end of Chapter 4-Questions to Ask When Selecting a Lender) can save you up to $1,000 in lost fees. Even if you think that you know what you can afford, it's always better to get pre-approved with a lender in order to have this verified—before you write a sales contract, rather than after writing a contract when your money is already at risk. To confirm your buying power, apply with a licensed mortgage originator. Use my "Questions to Ask When Selecting A Lender" Checklist at the end of Chapter 4 as your guide.

3 Monumental Mortgage Money Mistakes to Avoid

1. Not getting pre-approved
2. Not understanding your loan options
3. Not planning/asking the right questions

1. Not Getting Pre-Approved

This can easily cost you $1000 right off the bat. Ugh! Not fun for your wallet. Lets say that you go home-shopping and make an offer on a new home and you are pre-qualified, but not pre-approved. If the lender calculates your income differently than you did during the pre-qualification process, you may not be on the same page when it comes to actually closing the loan. Watch out! That puts your earnest money deposit (aka binder) in jeopardy and can cost you home inspection and appraisal fees. Appraisal, home, and pest inspections can easily total $750-$1,000.

2. Not Understanding Your Loan Options

What down payment options do you have? Will a small difference in down payment equate to saving, or paying, tens of thousands in monthly mortgage insurance? What about property type and foreclosure properties? There are certain loans that are for those properties and certain loans that are not for foreclosures and condos. What if you made an offer on a HomePath (Fannie Mae Owned) property, but your lender didn't offer that type of loan? What will that cost you? Higher down payment, unnecessary appraisal costs, and, possibly higher mortgage insurance; again this can be $1,000s that you don't have to spend! See Chapter 13 for a full discussion on Loan Programs, and Chapter 15 for a full discussion on Loan Terms.

3. Not Planning/Asking the Right Questions

How much seller credit can you receive for which loan types? What? Yes, certain loans allow for maximum seller help for your purchase. For example, FHA allows for 6% seller help, while a conventional loan allows for 3% for a primary residence and only 2% for an investment property. These are important discussions to have with your lender before your real estate agent writes up your contract offer to the seller. Let's say you could have gotten 6%, but didn't know and you left $1,000's on the table and then used your money instead of the seller's? Bummer!

$$3$$

What is a Mortgage?

A mortgage is basically a loan to buy a house. When you apply for a mortgage, you are asking someone else to give you money to buy a home. What are the reasons you would ask someone else to give you money to buy a house? Maybe because you don't have your own money to pay cash for the property; maybe because you want to leverage the cash you do have by keeping it in your bank account; maybe you want to use the money for something else; maybe because you want an income tax deduction. Whatever your reason, this book is designed to help you navigate a system of regulations and requirements that has drastically changed in the past few years.

"Mort" in mortgage comes from the Latin and Old French "death." In Old French, "gage" is pledge. In the U.S. we are privileged to have 30-year mortgage terms; quite a long time. But, don't panic, most people sell or refinance every 4 years, not 30. And, life expectancies have changed quite a bit over the centuries! A 30-year mortgage could lead you to paying off your home long before retirement, especially if you pay a little extra each month to pay off your principal early.

Choosing to Get a Mortgage

Once you have decided that you want to purchase a home by getting a mortgage, the process is very easy if you are working with a lender that is working for you, with your best interests in mind. If you have picked up this mortgage guide, you have decided that you are ready to get a mortgage, that you would like to learn how to get ready for a mortgage, or would like to develop a timeline for getting a mortgage.

Why They "Give" You Money

Why would a lending institution give you money to buy a house? They think you are a good credit risk. What does that mean? They think you are going to pay them back the money. And, in the unlikely event that you do not make your mortgage payments, they believe that the home you have chosen is a secure investment to back the funds they have given you. The government now provides oversight and regulation of credit risk decisions made by lending institutions. The criteria on which the lenders base their decisions consists of pages and pages of details, such as debt-to-income ratio, credit score, court judgments, income, assets, loan-to-value, type of dwelling, length of the loan — just to name a few. There's also payment shock, down payment, sales price and type of loan (conventional, VA, FHA, USDA). Let's be clear, though. The lender is not "giving" you anything. The lender is loaning you money, backed by real estate collateral.

Getting the Money for Your Home

What do you have to give the lending institution to get them to loan you money to buy a house? Holy cow— you have to give them a ton of documents! And, you need to give them exactly what they ask for— no more, no less, and, in the form they need it. The lending institution will also make sure that the home you choose is a sound investment according to their underwriting standards, which will require different types of inspections based on the mortgage type you choose.

In Chapter 9, I will help you understand how the type of property you choose can affect your mortgage, and, in Chapter 11, I will outline the best way to submit documents, which documents are a must and how to find them— and how to do this in a way that will not delay the mortgage application process.

What You'll Be Paying Back

Once you've purchased a home with a mortgage, you'll be making a payment every month until your mortgage is paid off. It's not just the loan you'll be paying for every month. Your mortgage payment may include other required payments associated with buying a home.

Four categories comprise your monthly payment: Principal (the loan amount); Interest (the cost of getting a loan); Taxes (on the property for which you've gotten the loan); and, Insurance (for the property and/or the mortgage itself). These four categories are referred to as the PITI. Every month you will make one payment that includes PITI. You'll get more detail about PITI in Chapter 7.

The Future of Your Loan

Who will service your loan? Wait, what in the world is "service your loan"? The loan servicer is the institution that collects your monthly payments. The servicer may also hold and distribute your escrows (usually homeowners insurance and property taxes). The loan servicer may or may not be the same company that originated your mortgage and helped you buy your dream home.

Who will you communicate with after you have closed on your house? You will usually communicate with your loan servicer, but, a good mortgage banker is always happy to help you. Who can help you with future questions during the years you are making payments on your mortgage? Usually your loan servicer will be available to answer questions during your payment years. But, again, a good mortgage banker is always happy to help you, long after closing day.

Making Sense of the Jargon

Escrow
Collected at the time of closing, these are the funds that the mortgagee (lender) holds for you to make payments on your behalf. These funds are for property taxes and homeowners insurance. The mortgagee pays these bills annually, on your behalf. Usually, the lender will require an insurance payment for the coming year at closing, then money for insurance is collected every month as part of your mortgage payment. The lender sets aside this money to make your insurance and property tax payments when they are due annually.

Some loans allow you to choose not to escrow property taxes and homeowners insurance; in that case, you are responsible to make these payments yourself. In addition, if your loan allows you the option not to escrow, there is usually an additional fee. That fee can be paid on the HUD-1 (see Chapter 20 for more details) at the time of closing, or, it can result in a slightly higher interest rate. The reason the lenders charge a fee for you to assume responsibility for your own bill payment is because nonpayment of property taxes can result in a lien against the property, jeopardizing the lender's ability to collect repayment in the event of default (if you stop making your mortgage payment). Not paying homeowners insurance through escrow also puts the lender at risk. If you assume responsibility to make homeowners insurance payments, but then don't or fall behind, the lender and you both are at risk should something happen to your home. This demonstrates that all pricing (fees and interest rates) is risk-based. The higher the risk, the higher the price.

Payment Shock

The percentage of increase (difference) in your current rent or mortgage payment in comparison to the payment amount for the mortgage for which you are applying. For example, if you are currently paying $1,000 in rent, and the house you want to buy would require a $2,000 mortgage payment, the payment shock would be 100 percent. That payment shock number will be reviewed by the underwriter and would be a cause for concern. If you would be going from a $2500 rent payment to a $2000 mortgage payment, the underwriter would view that as a positive payment change. Payment shock is a risk level measured by the lender during the underwriting process.

Payoff Amount

Usually related to refinancing a home, this is the amount due on the current loan or loans (if you have a second mortgage). If you are refinancing, your new loan pays off the old loan or loans based on the current point of repayment in your amortization schedule. If you are selling your home, the payoff amount is the amount due to the lender to release your home (the collateral for the loan).

Property Tax Changes

The annual amount due for property tax can change based on the value of your home as assessed by your local property tax assessor. If your state allows you to homestead, there may be certain deductions or credits that you can apply for to reduce the amount of property taxes that you pay. Homesteading may also dictate the number of times per year that your property taxes are due— biannually or annually. Homesteading may also allow for a cap on the amount of property tax you must pay. Homestead qualifications and privileges vary by the state you live in. Be sure to ask your lender and real estate agent where to learn more about homesteading. It's usually free and is a benefit to you as a homeowner. However, homesteading is not an option in some states; it is a tax relief and or home protection program that some states use to benefit the homeowner and tax paying citizens.

If you are escrowing your property taxes and there is a change in your property tax amount due after closing, the lender will usually give you choices on how to make up the difference if your taxes are higher. For example, if your annual property tax rises from $4,000 to $5,000, the lender may allow you to either write a check for $1,000, or, increase your monthly escrow to cover the increase. This would increase your mortgage payment, but, you would not have to make the lump sum payment of $1,000. This is an example of how mortgage payments can change over time even if you have a fixed interest rate. If your property tax decreases, the loan servicer must refund you the difference in the amount of property tax due above and beyond the 5-month cushion and the amount they collected from you through the monthly escrow.

Homeowners Insurance Changes

Much the same as property tax changes, when your homeowners insurance payments change, the difference must be settled with your lender either by writing a check or changing your monthly escrow amount. Unlike property taxes, you can actually shop your insurance. If your insurance payments are raised, you may be able to get a better rate from a different company. When FEMA updates their flood hazard maps, some homeowners suddenly find themselves in a flood zone. For those still holding a mortgage on their homes, either a large lump sum is due because of the insurance requirements, or their monthly escrow increases. When flood insurance is not required, it is much less expensive to add that protection to your homeowners insurance package than when flood insurance is required.

$$\textcircled{4}$$

Decoding Lending Institutions

Who or What is a Lending Institution?

Who is the someone else that will loan you money to buy a home?
Usually you are asking a lending institution to loan you money.
A lending institution could be a bank insured by FDIC, a local
community bank, a private bank, a mortgage banker, or a mortgage
broker. While most banks have to adhere to the government policies
that govern the mortgage industry, some have more flexibility than
others. What are the differences between all of these institutions; why
should you choose one over the other?

Mortgage Bankers

A mortgage banker should have the expertise of the mortgage broker
and in-house underwriting like a bank. Mortgage bankers typically have
more products than regular banks. And of course since it's all they do,
a mortgage banker is extremely skilled at getting you to closing (which
is what you want). Mortgage bankers are focused on and committed to
mortgages; they do not see your mortgage application as a way to try to
sell you checking/savings/CD accounts, or any other product or service.
Mortgage bankers have an array of mortgage options available in-house;
they should not have to shop your loan to outside companies to find the
best program suited to your mortgage needs.

Mortgage bankers generally have a vast working knowledge of
the mortgage process and can contact their in-house processors

and underwriters directly, enabling more clear and consistent communication throughout the mortgage process. Since they are communicating with processors and underwriters within their own company, mortgage bankers have an advantage of streamlined communication and working relationships with key players in different departments that oversee your loan from application, to origination, to underwriting, to closing in a timely manner.

Mortgage Brokers

A mortgage broker usually has the most options. A mortgage broker is a loan specialist (this is all they do – they don't sell you checking/savings/CD accounts like mortgage specialists at big banks) and is usually very skilled in the loan process and loan terms. The mortgage broker is an intermediary and originates your loan. The mortgage broker qualifies you for a loan, originates the loan, and begins processing your loan. Mortgage brokers shop to find you the best loan product and best price for you; they have the most flexibility because they are not tied to any one bank or mortgage company. They have the freedom to find the best deal for you. The mortgage broker submits your loan to the lender who will underwrite, close, and fund your loan. The mortgage broker remains your direct line of communication to the lender throughout the loan process.

Mortgage brokers should have a skilled expertise of the mortgage process and stay in direct contact with the lender selected, enabling clear and consistent communication throughout the mortgage process. Although mortgage brokers work with out-of-house underwriters, to be successful they must have professional relationships in place with the lenders that they broker your loan to; be sure to ask your mortgage broker to make sure this is the case. *However, since the loan is not actually being approved by the mortgage broker, this leaves mortgage brokers with the least control.*

Banks

Banks are more rigid because they typically have stricter guidelines and less local flexibility, though the licensing guidelines for bank employees involved in the mortgage process are not as strict as mortgage brokers and mortgage bankers. Usually larger national banks will have more control over underwriting (because they have in-house underwriting), but the mortgage process moves more slowly in closing loans, sometimes double the time of a mortgage broker or mortgage banker. Gone are the days when you can walk into such banks and sit down with a loan officer to discuss your options. If you ask the teller of a larger bank to assist you with a mortgage, most likely they will give you an 800# to call. This will be the extent of your customer service. Consider the service you want in what will probably be the largest purchase of your entire life.

A locally owned community bank may have more flexibility than larger banks in their underwriting; they may be able to allow special exceptions because of their knowledge of and connection to the local community. A locally owned bank or credit union may be privately owned and able to make special exceptions based on deposits kept with that bank or based on past relationships with that customer. However, smaller banks usually have very strict underwriting guidelines for traditional financing and may not have as many mortgage options to offer you. A lot of smaller banks do not have the qualifications to carry government loans such as VA, FHA, and USDA, so they may have limited financing options available for you.

A "private client" or "wealth management" bank may be able to make special exceptions based on the net worth of a client and how much money a client keeps in deposits with that bank. But, be aware this is special preference given to the ultra-rich, whose deposits usually start in the millions.

Lending Institution Oversight
All lending institutions are overseen by the federal and state governments at some level and have lots of rules and restrictions to which they must adhere. All can be publicly or privately owned and operated. The key takeaway here is that they are all subject to similar regulations, *so make your choice based on the best loan options for you, the professional expertise and knowledge of your licensed loan officer, and ratings and reviews from third party sources such as the Better Business Bureau and online customer reviews from websites such as Zillow or Google.*

The Best Mortgage Tip

Why Shopping for the Best Current Mortgage Rate is a Huge Mistake

The key is to shop for the best lender, not the best rate. The best lender will be licensed, knowledgeable, and have access to the best mortgages and loan programs available for you. And they'll have the best rates. One company might tell you they have the lowest rate, and that may be true, but they may add on fees that make your loan even more expensive than a mortgage from another lender that has a rate that's slightly higher, but an overall loan cost that is significantly lower. By significantly lower, we're talking thousands of dollars, even tens of thousands of dollars. Be careful! Sometimes the interest rate is used as a hook. The integrity of the loan officer and the lending institution you choose can determine the cost of your loan even more so than the interest rate of your loan.

Think of it like car shopping— comparing a car to a mortgage (not a house)—because the cost of the mortgage is the product for which you are shopping. You don't just walk onto the floor of the Porsche dealership and ask for their best price on a Porsche 911, do you? Probably not, unless you've owned a Porsche before and know how much it costs for the exact specifications, and, what the maintenance and insurance for the car will cost you annually. A Porsche 911 is great if you don't drive in city traffic much and only need a two-seater. So, if you get the best price on a Porsche, but it doesn't meet your needs, how does that fit with your life? Did you get the best model for you? Color? Payment? Stereo? Seats? Model? Engine? Although the Porsche looked awesome and you were told you got the best price, did you get the best price out of all of the car options, or just the best price on the Porsche 911?

A mortgage is similar. You have many options depending on your credit score (this affects your rate differently with different loan programs), down payment, type of property you want to buy, how long you plan to stay in the house and much, much more. Some loans have government funding fees, some don't. How does that affect your monthly payment? How does it affect your investment? What if you got the lowest interest rate, but the highest mortgage insurance? Ouch! Is the mortgage insurance for the life of the loan, or, until you have 22% equity in the home? All these factors are critical in getting the best mortgage for YOU.

So, do your research and shop for the best lender. Ask friends and family members how their mortgage experience was when they bought a house. This should be recently, in the past two years or less as many things change often in the lending world. Ask them if they were happy with the loan options presented to them when they met with their lender. Ask them if they were pleased with the communication during the mortgage process. Did their lender attend the closing? Did their lender communicate clearly with them and answer all their questions to their satisfaction? This is the biggest purchase of your life! Make sure you are working with the best team that understands your goals and has the means to get you to where you want to go. Check out our checklist for shopping to find the best lender.

The Checklist

Questions to ask when selecting a lender:

❏ What type of license do you have?

❏ What are your credentials?

❏ What references do you have?

❏ Do you have a direct line? Or, will I call the 800# and be routed to the next available customer service representative?

❏ Will I deal with you directly for the entire mortgage process?

❏ How many other people will I work with at your company?

❏ How long have you been in the mortgage industry?

❏ What is your percentage of closed loans?

❏ What is your success ratio of closing loans on time?

❏ Do you have client surveys you can send me? Do you have third party reviews available online?

❏ What are the upfront costs I will incur before closing?

❏ Do you attend the closing to ensure there are no surprises and that my loan funds at closing?

❏ How long has your company been in business? How long has your company been closing mortgages?

❏ What is your rating with the Better Business Bureau? Locally & Nationally?

❏ Not all lenders can close your loan in 30 days or less. It's critical to ask this question of your lender BEFORE you start the loan process with them.

$$5$$

4 Keys to Qualifying for a Mortgage

There are four key qualifications for a mortgage. This set of qualifications used to be called the 4 Cs of mortgage lending — credit, capacity, capital, and, collateral. Instead of the 4 Cs, think about the 4 Key Qualifications to getting a mortgage in easy terms: Credit; Income & DTI; Assets & Down Payment; and, your new home. These four categories are the basis for any mortgage. Each of these plays a critical role in the likelihood and ability of the borrower (that's you!) to repay the debt. It may sound complicated now, but I will give you a working knowledge of these four concepts; understanding them will help you during your loan process so that you will know why your lender is asking for certain information and documentation— "Where's your paperwork, Wazowski!?"

I have some people say to me that they have excellent credit. Great! We love borrowers with excellent credit. That's a very important piece of the puzzle. But sometimes these borrowers don't realize that they also still need to show that they have the income to repay the debt. Pretty important, don't ya think? So, all 4 pieces of information are critical for loan approval.

Key Qualification #1 - Credit

Past credit is a good predictor of future behavior. If you have a history of not paying your bills, unless you have a big life change, you will probably not pay at least some of them in the future. The same goes for good credit. If you have a history of paying your bills on time, you are likely to do the same in the future. If you have limited or no credit history, that is also taken into consideration.

People often make the mistake of thinking that credit score is all that matters with credit. What's more important is why your credit score is the number it is. For example, is your credit score a 700 because you are young and have a few accounts that you have been paying on time for a couple of years? Or, is your credit score 700 because you had an excellent credit history for 10 years, but you had a bankruptcy 3 years ago and are just rebuilding your credit? Is your credit score a 700 because you had a great history of paying 4 tradelines (car payment, one student loan, and, two credit cards) on time for 3 or more years, but you missed a medical bill and it was sent to collections?

Hmmmm, do you see the difference between each example? So, your credit score number is important, but why your credit score "is what it is" is really what the lender is reviewing. Also, while credit is important, the other critical parts of loan qualification we are discussing are just as important. Sometimes people tell me that they have an 800 credit score and that's all I need to know to qualify them. That's not true. If you have an 800 credit score, but are unemployed, you probably will not qualify for a mortgage. We'll get more into Credit later in Chapter 6.

Key Qualification #2 – Income & DTI

How about Income? Your income needs to be verified to make sure you can repay the loan. Your income is used to calculate your debt-to-income ratios. So, it's not just your income that the lender is looking for; the lender needs your income to calculate your risk based on your income in comparison to other debts. Debt-to-income ratio is critical for loan approval. This is one of the reasons that the lender verifies your Federal Income Tax returns and 1099s or W2s. The lender wants to make sure you are making enough money to repay your mortgage, along with your other monthly bills.

Let's look at debt-to-income ratio through an example. If your adjusted gross annual income is $100,000, but your monthly debts equal your monthly income, would it be a good idea for the lender to approve you for a mortgage that will create additional debt and another monthly payment for you? What are the odds you will repay that debt? Or, will you default on the other debt for which you are already responsible?

Yep, you guessed it — probably not so good for you or for the bank investing in you for your home purchase.

Debt-to-income ratios include front-end and back-end ratios, also called top and bottom ratios. The front-end (top) ratio is your new estimated total mortgage payment (PITI—principal, interest, taxes, and insurance) divided by your monthly income. If your new total mortgage payment is $2,500 and your adjusted gross monthly income is $9,000, your front-end ratio is 27.8 percent. Your adjusted gross monthly income is Line 37 on your federal tax return. It includes your household income minus tax deductions.

Your back-end (bottom) ratio is your total monthly debts plus your new estimated total mortgage payment, divided by your monthly income. Typically health insurance, auto insurance, mobile phone bills, and electric bills do not report on your credit, so you may qualify for a payment that you are not comfortable paying each month. So be sure to think about all of your monthly obligations and make sure that you are comfortable with the mortgage payment amount that comes from your pre-qualification and also from your final loan approval. If you are not comfortable with the monthly mortgage payment, talk to your lender.

For more specifics, read about loan programs in Chapter 13 and the full discussion of DTI in Chapter 7.

Key Qualification #3 – Assets & Down Payment

Assets are liquid and non-liquid property that you own, minus any debts against each listed asset. For example — your car (minus your car loan if you have one), checking and savings accounts, 401K, 403B, IRA, Roth IRA, money market or certificate of deposit (CD), homes (minus the mortgages against them), and, life insurance policies are considered assets. Assets must be verified. One reason for verification is to make sure the down payment and any closing costs you are responsible for paying are coming from your own funds and are not a gift. We'll talk more about gifts later in this book. If the funds are not yours and are not a gift, a payment must be calculated as if those assets are a loan. Worse! It might disqualify you from loan approval.

Assets must also be verified to meet reserve requirements for some loans. When you are buying a primary residence, usually two months of reserves must be verified. When you are purchasing an investment property, the requirement is usually six months of reserves for each investment property owned plus two months of reserves for your primary residence (if applicable). The amount of reserves per month equals your total monthly PITI for each property.

Let's talk about assets for a minute and how assets relate to loan risk. Do you think you are more likely to keep paying a debt if you have more invested? For example, if you make a $0 down payment on a home versus the scenario of making a $50,000 down payment on a home, which mortgage are you more likely to repay? Will you choose the loan in which you have invested $50,000, or, the loan in which you have invested $0? Ding, ding, ding! You guessed right again! The loan for the home in which you have invested $50,000 of your own cash!

So, your assets are an important part of your loan approval process. Four parts of your home purchase come from your assets — your binder deposit, your down payment, your closing costs, and your reserves. The lender will assess your total assets, and also how your assets will be applied to your home purchase during the purchase process. This is one of the reasons why lenders have to verify and source your assets.

The binder, also called earnest money deposit, is another way you will use your assets. When your contract on a home is accepted, you will be asked to submit an earnest money deposit with your sales contract. That earnest money deposit binds the contract; the required amount is typically between 1 to 3 percent of your sales price. If you don't perform according to your sales contract, your binder is at risk — keeping your earnest money is at the seller's discretion. At closing, your binder is applied to all of the fees incurred in the loan process, as well as to your down payment.

The down payment is calculated as a percentage of the sales price or the appraised value, whichever is lower. The percent of down payment required varies by the type of loan. Some loans, such as USDA or VA, currently do not require a down payment. Currently FHA requires as little 3.5% down payment. Conventional financing down payments vary based on the type of residence. (For specific information about loan program requirements, see Chapter 13 Loan Programs and Chapter 14 VA Loans.) Do you intend to occupy the home as your primary residence? Will it be a second home? Will it be an investment property?

There are also down payment assistance programs that may be available to help you with the down payment. These are usually based on income, geography and credit score. It's a good idea to do some research on your own, as well as ask your licensed loan officer what is available in your area. Sometimes if state or Federal grants are a possibility, particular government grants may be out of funding depending on the time of year. This is because funding grants may change, and because grant money sometimes runs out and might not again be available until the next fiscal year. Also, not all lenders are familiar with what's available. Be sure to ask about ALL the loan programs, grants, and assistance for which you may qualify.

The down payment made from your assets reduces your loan amount and also becomes all or part of your equity in the property. Typically, the larger the down payment, the stronger the loan application. But, just to mix it up, some government loan types do not require a down payment, so in those cases you can have a strong loan application with no down payment. When you make a larger down payment to reduce your loan amount, your monthly principal and interest payment is reduced. Sometimes a slightly larger down payment can make the difference on whether or not your loan is approved. Sometimes making a larger down payment is not a benefit because it only slightly reduces your total monthly payment, therefore keeping the cash in your reserves is more beneficial. Talk to your loan officer about the advantages and disadvantages of various down payment amounts.

Closing costs are the fees required to close on your loan, the fees charged by the various entities that work for you to buy or refinance your home. Closing costs are also paid from your assets. Most closing costs are paid on closing day. However, typical fees paid in advance as part of your loan are home inspection, pest inspection, appraisal, and, estoppel fee. Fees paid on closing day are fees to your lender, fees to your real estate agent (usually paid by the seller), fees paid to the title company, fees paid to the state and county where you are purchasing the home, homeowners insurance, up-front mortgage insurance (if required), and, escrows. Remember your binder will cover some or even all of these fees. Keep in touch with your lender throughout the process so that you have an idea of how much money you will need to bring to the table on closing day. (For more detailed information about closing costs, see Chapter 20 Closing)

Your reserves are your cushion money if your income is reduced. The lender needs to know that you can still make your mortgage payment in the event of temporary income changes. Typically for a primary residence, two months of reserves are required; for each investment property, six months of reserves are required. Any reserves over and above make your loan position stronger. Keep in mind that your reserves are calculated from your assets after your binder, down payment, and closing costs are all subtracted.

Key Qualification #4 – Your New Property

Not all property is created equal. Your dream home may be a single family home in the suburbs, it may be a condo in the city, a townhouse, a co-op, beach house on the ocean, or, a townhouse in a planned unit development. Lenders view property types differently and you should be aware of this fact. There are a variety of different requirements that each lender has based on the property type. Down payments may vary based on property types. Loan programs have different requirements based on property type. It's important to discuss this with your lender and ask questions. Let your lender know what property types you are considering so there are no surprises later.

The Checklist

Top 7 Massive Mistakes to Avoid That Could Prevent You from Getting Approved for a Mortgage

❏ Don't buy or lease an automobile!

❏ Don't move assets from one bank account to another!

❏ Don't change jobs!

❏ Don't buy new furniture or major appliances for your new home!

❏ Don't run a credit report on yourself!

❏ Don't attempt to consolidate bills before speaking with your lender!

❏ Don't pack or ship information needed for the loan application!

Seems like a pretty simple list, huh? You might be surprised by the number of people that don't heed this advice, then become absolutely stunned when they can't close on their new home because they have made one of the 7 massive mistakes listed above. Some people heed this advice for a while, but then think that it couldn't possibly matter if they go buy new furniture for their new home the day before closing. It's the day before closing — everything is all set, right? Not true! Your credit is monitored right up until closing, and if you make one of these mistakes your debt-to-income ratio could hit the tipping point to disqualify you for your mortgage. Though I touch on all of these important concepts throughout the book, keep reading here for a more detailed explanation of how these mistakes can jeopardize your mortgage.

Don't buy or lease an automobile!

This can create a big problem for several reasons. One, it can drop your credit score. When you are shopping for a car loan or any other loan, one or more creditors are pulling your credit. That alone can drop your score depending on how many creditors and over what time frame your credit is pulled. Two, when the new line of credit is opened for a car loan, the loan starts at the maximum amount. So, once it shows up on your credit report, it starts at the maximum debt allowed which also affects your credit score negatively.

Another area that is affected by this new credit line is your debt-to-income ratio. Lenders look carefully at your debt-to-income ratio. A large payment such as a car lease or purchase can greatly impact those ratios and prevent you from qualifying for a home loan. The new debt is calculated into your debt-to-income ratio. Specifically, what lenders call your "back end" or "bottom" debt-to-income ratio. If your ratio is too high for your loan type, the new payment may disqualify you for the loan. Example: I was working with clients who had a debt-to-income ratio that was at 39%, and a credit score of 740 when they applied for their loan. They found their dream house, made an offer which was accepted, and we were on our way to closing! They decided that along with their new house they would like to get a shiny new car to put in the garage of their new home. Who wouldn't, right? Well, unfortunately, their new car payment brought their monthly debt-to-income ratio to 46% and disqualified them for the loan. Not a very happy ending, but a great example of a massive mortgage mistake to avoid for a smooth easy closing.

What to do: Always consult your licensed loan officer before obtaining any new debt while you are in the process of obtaining a mortgage loan or while you are being pre-qualified for a mortgage loan. The days of buying a new car at the same time you buy your new house are gone. With lenders monitoring your credit 24/7, they know when you apply for credit and have to do a credit supplement showing your new payment for each new line of credit. This means more paperwork and time delays for you! All this gets added into your debt-to-income ratio.

Don't move assets from one bank account to another!

These transfers show up as new deposits and complicate the application process because you must then disclose and document the source of funds for each new account. The lender can verify each account as it currently exists. You can consolidate your accounts later if you need to. Since you need to source all deposits over $500 (on average), any deposits that cannot be sourced cannot be used for your down payment, nor your closing costs. If those are the only funds you have, the lender may not be able to close your loan so you can't buy your new home! You may think that moving all your money into one account before closing is a good idea. Maybe, maybe not. It depends on where your money was before you moved it. In many cases this can open a whole new can of worms for you and your lender to document. Consult your lender before moving any funds during the loan process.

Don't change jobs!

A new job may involve a probation period, which must be satisfied before income from the new job can be considered for qualifying purposes. According to Fannie Mae & Freddie Mac (we will talk more about them in more detail later), you must have at least 30 days of employment in order to use that W2 job as income. If you are 1099 or on commission, you will need to wait at least one year before the lender can use that income to qualify you for the loan. This doesn't mean you can't get a new job and buy a home. You just need to make sure you have clear communication with your lender and real estate agent regarding the timing of your closing, especially when you write your sales contract.

Don't buy new furniture or major appliances for your new home!

If the new purchases increase the amount of debt you are responsible for on a monthly basis... there is the possibility this may disqualify you from getting the loan, or reduce the available funds you need to meet closing costs. I know it seems like buying furniture for your new home is normal, but you must WAIT until after closing! Any new payments for furniture or appliances must be counted in your debt-to-income ratio and may disqualify you for the loan. For example, let's say your back end monthly debt-to-income ratio is 41% which is the maximum for an FHA loan. If you add a $20.00 monthly payment for a new TV on a payment plan from Best Buy, you may have just disqualified yourself from closing the loan for your new home. Another example might be that you have decided to pay cash for your new high efficiency washer and dryer. If you needed those funds for closing costs and down payment, again you have disqualified yourself from closing the loan for your new home.

Don't run a credit report on yourself!

This will show as an inquiry on your lender's credit report. Inquiries must be explained in writing. The loan process can be stressful enough! Don't add another reason to supply more paperwork. Your lender will be happy to give you a copy of your credit report.

Don't attempt to consolidate bills before speaking with your lender!

The lender can advise you if this needs to be done. This is where the over achievers can unknowingly sabotage their own loan. While it can be a great idea to consolidate debt, find a trusted lender who can advise you how to do this properly so that it does not impact your loan application in a negative manner.

Don't pack or ship information needed for the loan application!

These days most documents needed by the lender are available electronically, but be sure and check with your lender to find out which documents are needed at initial application as well as later during the loan process. For example, not all lenders request tax returns and W2s at the beginning of the loan process. Rest assured you will need to supply these documents before you close on your new loan, so don't pack personal tax returns, business tax returns, W2s, 1099s, homeowners insurance and property tax documents, student loan papers, divorce decrees, death certificates, bankruptcy or other critical documentation when you move.

⑥

Understanding Credit

Credit score is critical—but so are the elements comprising the credit score. You can have a 720 credit score, but if you had a foreclosure last year, the likelihood of you getting approved for a traditional loan is slim to none. Credit is a fluid thing. You can have great credit this month, but if you stop paying your bills and have a tax lien show up on your credit, all of a sudden you will have bad credit.

If you have bad credit and work to repair it, pay your bills on time, and utilize credit responsibly, it will take some time, but you can eventually have good credit. Sounds basic, but if you pay your bills on time—that's good; if you pay your bills late or not at all—that's bad. The more often you pay your bills late, the more it hurts your credit score. Also, the later you pay, the more your credit score is hurt; paying 90 days late is much worse than paying 30 days late.

Different types of events affect credit in various ways. For example, length of credit comprises about 10% of your credit score. This is great for those of you who have used credit responsibly for years. For those of you who are younger, don't despair; there are some tricks around this. But also keep in mind—length of credit is only about 10% of your credit score, so focus on the other 90% of the credit score components.

Major life events can have big impacts on credit scores. A divorce, for example, may involve late payments on mortgage payments and car payments while things get sorted out. A house may go into foreclosure due to a divorce or loss of income. We see many loan applications with recent short sales or foreclosures due to the real estate and market crash of 2007 (yes, it's still affecting people, years later). All of these will impact your credit. If you used to have high balances on credit cards and have paid them down—good for you! This will help your credit score. But if at the same time a collection from your ex-spouse shows up on your credit, it may cancel out the lower credit card balance. See how credit is ever changing? Here are more in depth examples about how lenders look at your credit.

Foreclosures & Short Sales

I have people tell me all the time that they make plenty of money, have lots of money to put down, and are shocked when the banks don't want to lend them money because they just had a foreclosure last year. FHA loans currently require that 3 years have passed since a short sale before you are eligible for an FHA loan. Different loan programs have different requirements. For example, for a conventional loan, 4 years must have passed since a short sale in order to qualify for that loan type. But, for a VA loan sometimes an exception can be made that allows for 2 years since a foreclosure. And, things are always changing.

At the beginning of 2014, conventional mortgages required at least two years since a short sale (if you were current on your payment at the time of the short sale) for you to be eligible for 80% financing. So, you had to put at least 20% as a down payment. In order to put down less of a down payment for conventional financing, you must wait longer. As of August 2014, this is no longer the case. Now a conventional mortgage requires a 4-year waiting period from the time of your short sale. This is an example of how quickly mortgage guidelines and regulations can change.

Bankruptcy

Bankruptcy is governed by federal law. Basically, when your debt load is too overwhelming, you can file for bankruptcy. Currently one of the most common reasons for bankruptcy is unpaid medical bills; bankruptcy is also common when people face divorce, job loss, or other major life challenges. Filing for bankruptcy means that you will go through the courts to legally manage your debt—either writing it off completely or setting up a repayment strategy that will be monitored by the court. When your debts are "written off" through a bankruptcy court, your debt doesn't just disappear for free. There's a price that you will pay into the future for quite sometime; that price is your new label as a high or bad risk for loans and credit. The rules of how your credit is written-off or managed vary by the type of bankruptcy. The two types most commonly associated with mortgages are Chapter 7 and Chapter 13 bankruptcies.

People generally use a Chapter 7 Bankruptcy claim when they feel that their debt burden is so great they will never be able to repay the debt or recover financially. Under the Chapter 7 Bankruptcy, some assets are liquidated to pay the creditors, and certain property is exempt from liquidation. The bankruptcy reflects on credit scores negatively, but does allow a person to get free from the debt burden. Chapter 7 Bankruptcy claims remain on your credit report for up to ten years, though you can usually begin getting loans or credit within two years or less. But the bankruptcy may subject you to sub-prime lending rates and higher interest rates for credit cards, if you are able to qualify. Generally, people that have had a Chapter 7 Bankruptcy can begin getting credit cards and loans sooner than those that file a Chapter 13 Bankruptcy.

Under a Chapter 13 Bankruptcy, the court oversees a payment plan established between the borrower and creditors. To keep any property affected by the bankruptcy, the borrower must abide by all repayment terms set by the court, and must do so within a set amount of time not to exceed 5 years. Under a Chapter 13, you are not allowed to get credit for new loans or credit cards unless you have permission from the court. A Chapter 13 Bankruptcy remains on your credit report for up to ten years. A Chapter 13 Bankruptcy will allow you to avoid foreclosure and keep your home as long as your home is included in your repayment schedule.

For more information go to uscourts.gov, navigate to the Federal Courts section, then navigate to the Bankruptcy section.

Judgments

Banks don't like these either. They must be paid in full and cleared before most lenders will allow you to borrow money for a mortgage. This is because judgments and liens may be attached to real estate if they are not paid. A judgment or lien may be tied to a property. That means that the judgment or lien must be satisfied in order for the property to be sold. The banks do not want anything to interfere with their ability to collect the repayment of the mortgage.

Tax Liens

Usually the only thing that can supersede a bank lien is a federal tax lien. This may prevent the lender from collecting their loan if you default on the mortgage. This is another one of the reasons that lenders verify your income taxes, to make sure you do not have any outstanding payments to the federal government. The lender always wants to make sure there is nothing in the way of your mortgage being repaid, such as another lien. Other liens against your property represent more risk for the lender. These types of liens negatively affect your credit.

Collections

A collection account is an account that is past due and the original creditor has assigned this account to a collection agency to recover the debt. This will still show up on your credit report for up to 7 years and reflects extremely negatively towards your credit standing. Collections demonstrate to the lender that you have a problem paying your bills. Whether it is your fault of not, this is another red flag to the lender. A pattern of collections will result in a lower credit score and some loan programs don't allow for any recent collections. But don't just rule out the possibility that you can get a mortgage if you have recently had collections; be sure to ask your licensed mortgage professional about loan options that may be available to you.

Credit Card Balances

The amount of open lines of credit and how recently those lines of credit were opened reflect in your credit score, along with your payment history. Credit balances usually account for about 30% of your credit score. How much of a balance you carry on your revolving lines of credit reflect on your credit score. It's best to keep a balance of 50% or less on your revolving lines of credit, such as credit cards, house accounts, and, home equity loans. The lower the percentage, the better — just don't make it zero. What? It's confusing, I know. You want to keep a small balance of 5%-10% just to show you are using the line of credit responsibly. If you have credit questions, just ask us at info@bestmortgagebook.com.

All of these credit factors are considered in calculation of the risk for the lender, as well as the government entities that back the mortgages (Fannie Mae and Freddie Mac). The banks are willing to take a calculated risk. A good predictor of future behavior is past behavior. If you just walked away from a mortgage, you are telling the lender upfront that you do not honor your credit commitments and are therefore a BIG risk. The banks like to make money, not lose it. People that walk away from mortgages are too big a risk for most lenders; regardless of how much money you make now, or funds you have available now, or how much cash you have for a down payment — if you have walked away from a mortgage in the past, you are a big risk.

Q&A Session

Q: Are there things people need to do to their credit before applying for a mortgage?

Elysia: Well, this is an interesting question. If you are already working with a credit repair specialist, then finish your goals before you apply. If you are not sure about your credit, then just apply. Just pull the Band-Aid off! One "pull" on your credit usually doesn't affect the score, in fact that car loan you got with your new car will drop your credit score about 10 times more than a mortgage inquiry. When you are shopping for a new car loan, usually the dealership shops your credit to several places to get you the best rate. That's multiple "pulls" on your credit. When you actually open the car loan it starts at the highest balance possible since that is what you were approved for. Unfortunately, the credit scoring models read this as a new line of credit that is maxed out, plus possibly multiple "pulls" on your credit. Ouch! A new car loan can drop your credit score anywhere from 40-60 points. So, don't worry about the mortgage company pulling your credit. It usually only drops it 5-10 points. It's what reports on your credit that affects your credit score the most.

Lots of people come to me and want to be pre-qualified, but don't want their credit pulled. Mortgages are loans for hundreds of thousands of dollars, so guesses and estimates about credit standing aren't going to cut it. All lenders are going to require access to your credit. Mortgage lending is not like used car lending… you know those predatory used car programs that don't care about your credit history and charge you outrageous fees and interest? That does not happen in the mortgage industry; it's highly regulated to protect you, the consumer. And lenders need to run your credit through a specific portal to protect the company and to protect you by giving you an accurate accounting of your eligibility. Again, guesswork is not acceptable in the mortgage industry; your ability to pay your mortgage must be documented in detail. Lenders don't look forward to house repos, they want you to stay in your home and successfully pay off your mortgage.

A: Well, what if I did run my credit already — why can't the mortgage company use that to pre-qualify me?

Elysia: Some people want to send me a credit report from a website they found through a search engine. Such websites can provide a great service for monitoring your credit. It can help you identify areas you can improve and help you check for accuracy on your credit report, which is very important. However, a mortgage lender cannot use reports from these websites to pre-qualify or pre-approve you for a loan. Those types of credit reports are not in the specialized format used by professionals in the banking and lending industries. In addition, the consumer/retail credit websites are not run on the same scoring platform as the lender, so the score is usually 30-50 points off (which is terribly misleading to the consumer who subscribes to those websites). Finally, these reports may not contain information that is required for a mortgage application, such as tradeline categories. Tradeline categories are the various types of credit lines, such as revolving lines of credit, installment loans, and mortgages.

Q: How much does it cost to have a lender run the proper credit report?

Elysia: Some lenders charge $75-$100 for a pre-qualification. Lots of work goes into a good pre-qualification or better yet, pre-approval. I find anything over $100 for an application fee a bit outrageous. Be careful, because some companies have hidden methods for charging fees before you get a loan. For example, I've heard of large banks and mortgage companies charging loan applicants at the time a good faith estimate is requested. They do this by charging the customer for the appraisal at $450, and won't release the good faith estimate until the applicant pays that charge.

We currently charge no fee for running a credit report. After running the credit report, if needed we can run a credit simulator to see if there is room for improvement on your credit score. We find that most borrowers that don't want their credit pulled have either been turned down by another lender and know they don't qualify, or, they aren't really serious about beginning the process.

This is the reason most banks now charge for pre-qualifications. Just like any other professional, lenders don't want to waste time if someone is not serious about getting a mortgage. You know how doctors, massage therapists, and hotels charge you if you don't show up? A lender isn't going to charge you for missing an appointment to discuss your loan application, but it is a frustrating waste of professional time. Remember, there is a team of specialized, certified, and trained professionals working hard on every mortgage, even just to take a look at your eligibility.

Q: Do people hurt their credit score if they run a credit report on themselves a month before applying for a mortgage?

Elysia: No, but it's pointless. Just have the lender run it as part of your loan application. The lender needs to evaluate your credit report with your loan application. If you want to get to your goal, you need a road map. With just credit or just your income, assets, and job history, the lender cannot fully evaluate your loan application.

Q: Mortgage brokers can't give financial advice, but what can they do to help people?

Elysia: A licensed loan officer can let people know what they can qualify to purchase by giving them a dollar amount of the most they are qualified to borrow. A skilled loan officer can let you know what do to so you can get qualified. This can be by improving your credit score, debt reduction, increasing assets or receiving a gift. There are many options if you are working with an experienced, licensed loan officer. If you don't currently qualify, a good loan officer can help you understand what you need to do to work towards qualifying for a mortgage in the future.

Q: What are the key concepts about credit in relation to getting a mortgage?

Elysia: Credit is evaluated to establish a baseline about your ability to repay. A credit report shows your past history. What did you pay on time? Do you have a history of over-extending your credit? Have you defaulted and not paid what you said you would pay in the past? Are there legal obligations (such as judgments) that you are responsible for and may not have disclosed? How much good credit do you have versus bad credit? How long ago was that collection? How much debt are you responsible for on a monthly basis and overall?

Q: How does the importance of credit differ with different loan types?

Elysia: With challenged credit, government loans, such as FHA, USDA, and VA, tend to be more forgiving than conventional loans. Conventional loans have more strict requirements for credit than government loans. Of course, due to our recent housing bubble (in case you are too young to remember or already blocked out 2007-2010) there have been significant changes in the credit requirements for time passed since bankruptcy and foreclosure.

The government loan programs have more flexibility since the United States Federal Government backs these programs. For goodness sake, the veterans and our military service men and women deserve all the benefits, and then some! For example, if you apply for a VA loan, if you had a foreclosure in the last two years, but have since established good credit, you can still qualify for 100% financing (no down payment). For conventional loan programs, you would have to wait at least four (may be up to seven!) years (as of August 2014) since the foreclosure, with good credit established, to put down a 20% down payment and qualify for 80% financing. See the difference? Let's put it in # and $ form…20% of $300,000= $60,000 down payment vs. $0. Not to mention the difference of waiting two to five more years before you can get a mortgage. This is just one example of the myriad of credit nuances between loan types.

Q: How does the importance of credit differ with different homes, if at all?

Elysia: Sometimes there are stricter credit requirements for condominium purchases and investment properties. But, generally speaking, for primary residences I haven't found that the importance of credit or the way credit is factored varies according to the property type.

Q: Who has a right to know your credit score? (Real estate agent? Seller?)

Elysia: No one — only you (and, of course, your lender). During the loan process, you are protected by the government through numerous laws and regulations such as the Gramm-Leach-Bliley Act and the Fair Credit Reporting Act. If these laws are violated, punishment can be fines and/or jail time. This is a good time for me to share that when your real estate agent asks you for a Good Faith Estimate (GFE), credit report, or any piece of your loan documents, you do NOT have to give it to her or him. Of all the documents in your loan package (1003, application, appraisal, disclosures, etc.), real estate agents are only allowed a copy of the HUD-1 Settlement Statement at closing. That's it.

But when real estate agents ask us for GFEs, that is a direct violation. That information is between you and your licensed mortgage professional. Do real estate agents know the details of your credit and income? Do you want them to? They are not bound by the same laws and regulations as your lender. But, if your real estate agent asks you for it, it's always a good idea to ask why. If your appraisal can help you negotiate a lower sales price and you want to give it to your real estate agent, that makes sense. The real estate agent's expertise is supposed to be helping you find the home of your dreams, negotiating the sales price, negotiating terms of the sales contract, and, then reviewing all of that with you so you are all (borrower, real estate agent, and mortgage professional) on the same page. That's a great exercise to do with both your real estate agent and lender so everyone knows the deadlines and is working together to achieve your goal of home ownership.

Q: Do you have any credit stories — success stories or beware stories?

Elysia: Always be upfront with your lender about any credit issues on your credit report, or any issues that you think may report on your credit in the future — so no one is blindsided. For example, if you know that your ex-spouse or ex-partner is going to be suing you for child support, but it just didn't hit your credit report yet, that would be a vital piece of information to share with your lender.

I was working with a couple that was almost to closing when a collection for child support showed up on their credit. For the particular loan type they were getting, collections within the past year were not allowed. Unfortunately, this new collection meant no loan for them. They had already spent over $1,000 on home inspections and an appraisal. That money was lost.

Also, since that was the only loan that they had qualified for, they were stuck renting for at least another year. Since they had already given notice to their current landlord that they were moving, they were also forced to find a new place to rent and move. The rental deposits, moving costs, appraisal, and home inspection are lost costs, probably several thousand dollars. This is not only costly, but also stressful. If they would have known about the child support and disclosed that to the lender up front, perhaps there might have been a different outcome.

Making Sense of the Jargon

"A" Loan or "A" Paper
A credit rating where the FICO score is 700 or above. There have been no late mortgage payments within a 12-month period. This is the best credit rating to have when entering into a new loan. This used to be 660 or so. Since the mortgage meltdown Fannie Mae & Freddie Mac are more strict about what they consider "good" credit. Both government entities have added "hits" to pricing for credit scores less than 720. That means that if your credit score is less than a 720 you will not get the best interest rate available for a conventional loan.
740+ is the top tier of A paper.

"B" Loan or "B" Paper
FICO scores from 620 – 659, no longer! Now B Paper is 640-700. You are current and on-time with 85% or better of your debts, no mortgage late payments and keep your credit balances at less than ½ of what you are able to spend.

"C" Loan or "C" Paper
Factors such as two 30-day late mortgage payments and two to three 30 day late installment loan payments in the last 12 months will put you in the C Paper category. No delinquencies over 60 days are allowed. There should be two to four years since a bankruptcy.

"D" Loan, "D" Paper, "D" Credit
Lenders and creditors refer to bad credit as "D" credit. It could be because you have a history of not paying bills, a foreclosure on your credit report, late payments, bankruptcy, default on student loans, tax liens, etc. The D score range is generally 500 to 619. Sub-prime lending rates refer to the higher interest rates imposed on people with D credit — these higher interest rates are because of the really high risk that

people with D credit scores will not repay the loan. Just remember that your credit is a snapshot in time. So, you could have great credit today, stop paying your bills tomorrow and have that show up on your credit report next month. On the other side of that coin, if you have a long history of not paying your debts and bills on time, there is still hope for you. You just have to establish good credit, clean up your bad credit, and then you may be able to qualify for a mortgage after a period of time. Ask your lender for suggestions on credit repair companies. There is an entire industry devoted to this very subject.

Charge-Off
A charge-off is a debt that the financial institution removes from their balance sheet and releases from your debt. A charge-off will still show up on your credit report for up to 7 years. This will affect your credit score negatively.

Co-Signed Account
An account on which there is more than one person legally responsible for payment.

Co-Signer
An additional person on a credit or loan application that agrees to equal responsibility for repayment of a loan or responsibility for lines of credit and credit cards.

Credit Bureau
Credit bureaus are regulated by the government and exist to provide information about how consumers utilize credit. Credit bureaus provide this information to lenders only with the consent of the borrower. The information is also available to consumers. By law, you are allowed one free credit report annually, from each of the three major bureaus. The three major bureaus are TransUnion, Equifax, and, Experian. Kroll is another credit bureau. Anytime a financial institution pulls your credit, you are entitled to receive a copy of the scores, even if you have already received your free annual report. If you are declined for credit, the lender must give you your scores and also notify you of the reason for denial within 60 days.

Credit Counseling & Credit Repair Companies
Credit counseling and credit repair are easy to get confused. There are non-profit companies that can help you develop a strategy for paying down debt. There are also for-profit credit repair companies that can safely help you repair your credit. A for-profit credit repair company

that will not get you into further trouble will remove incorrect data from your credit report.

Another type of safe credit counseling involves a third-party that helps you develop a credit management strategy that allows you to systematically pay off your debts, current and past. Be careful with this type of debt counseling because if you pay off old debt that has not recently reported to the credit bureaus, this can actually make old bad debt look like new bad debt, which may actually hurt your score more than help it.

Be sure to talk to your mortgage professional if you are thinking about using this type of credit counseling before applying for a mortgage. For example, if you have three collections showing up on your credit report, and one reported last month but the other two collections haven't sent anything to the credit bureaus in three years, the correct ethical action is to pay all three. But, this will have a mixed affect on your credit score. Paying off the recent collection will help your credit score; paying off the two old collections will hurt your score. It's possible to pay off the older debts after closing so that you can still adhere to your ethical standards of paying off your debts.

Beware of for-profit credit counseling companies. This involves a third-party company that puts together all of your debt and makes the payments for you, then you make payments to them. This looks horrible on your credit reports. Lenders view this as indicative of your inability to pay your bills on your own. Most loans will not be approved if you are currently having your debt managed by a credit counseling company.

And this one time...

I was working with a client last summer who was concerned about his credit. I reviewed his credit and let him know that at that time he qualified to purchase a property. He decided that he wanted to clean up his credit a bit before moving forward down the path to home ownership. A decision that I respected, but suggested he do after closing on his new home. He chose not to move forward with the purchase of a home and instead to focus on his credit.

In addition to paying down some loan balances, he also paid off some old collections. When he came back to me this summer all excited and ready to buy, his credit score no longer qualified. What? The collections that he paid off caused that old bad debt to read as new bad debt. He was so frustrated that he no longer qualified. It will take some time for that new bad debt to become history and his current responsible debt use to outweigh the bad that resurfaced.

...at mortgage camp.

Credit Grantor
This is just another term for the lender, the entity that is granting credit to you.

Credit History
Credit history is basically your credit report as generated by the credit bureaus. Your credit report is a compilation of your credit history.

Credit Report
A credit report is the information generated by the credit bureaus. A credit report can also include the addresses of places where you have lived, and, your work history. Credit reports may also include aliases. Credit reports contain 7-years of your credit history, addresses, and work history; your credit report may list up to 10-years of history if you have had a bankruptcy. All lenders pull a tri-merged credit report, which includes information from all three credit bureaus—Trans Union, Equifax, and Experian.

Credit Risk & Credit Worthiness
This is the term used by financial institutions to describe the probability that an applicant may default on a loan or extension of credit.

Credit Score
This is a calculation, determined by specific formulas, that is meant to predict the risk that the applicant will not repay debt. The lower the score, the higher the risk.

Credit Scoring
Credit scoring is done by the three credit bureaus. Each of those has a unique scoring model and use different models for different creditors. For example, your score may be different if you are applying for a

mortgage, versus applying for an auto loan, versus pulling your own credit score online.

Deed in Lieu

It's actually a Deed in Lieu of Foreclosure. This gives you and the lender a better option than foreclosure. It means that you give the title of the home back to the lender, and then the lender releases you from the debt and sells the home to recover your unpaid mortgage debt. It's better than foreclosure because it saves the borrower and the lender both time and money that would be spent in court under a foreclosure. It also reflects differently on a borrower's credit than a foreclosure would.

Default

This is when a borrower stops making payments to a creditor. When you have not paid for over 90 days, the lender may proceed with the legal rights afforded to them to begin foreclosure. Typically lenders do not do this until the 90-day mark. They usually prefer payment to foreclosing on the property.

Delinquency

This is another term for making late payments. If you do not pay your creditors on time, you are in delinquency and the creditor has the right to charge fees for late payment. On a mortgage payment, typical late terms are 5% after 15 days and 4% after 15 days for government loans. Also, some states prohibit more than 4% late charges.

Equal Credit Opportunity Act (ECOA)

Per federal law, creditors cannot discriminate on the basis of race, color, religion, national origin, sex, marital status, receipt of income from public assistance programs, or past exercising of rights under the Consumer Credit Protection Act.

Fair Credit Reporting Act

The Fair Credit Reporting Act protects an individual's privacy rights and ensures that the credit bureaus are fair and accurate.

For more information read more about ECOA and the Fair Credit Reporting Act on the Federal Trade Commission Consumer Information website, consumer.ftc.gov.

Forbearance

If you are late making payments, a lender may use forbearance rather than foreclosure. This means that the lender will agree to a repayment plan with you so that you may renew making payments and keep your home.

Foreclosure

Foreclosure is the process a lender may use to take property from a borrower if the borrower is in default. The lender takes the property and then sells it to recover the loan amount unpaid by the borrower. Foreclosure laws vary from state to state.

Inquiry

Anytime you or a lender requests your credit report from a credit bureau, it's a credit inquiry. If you have a lot of credit inquiries in a short period of time, your credit score may be lowered.

Liabilities

This is basically all of your debts or payments that are required of you. Some liabilities that people forget about are alimony and child support. Your monthly liabilities are usually calculated using the minimum monthly payments required — this includes credit cards, other mortgages, installment loans such as car payments, alimony, child support, store lines of credit, etc. This can also be a current or past due liability such as a collection, tax lien, or judgment.

Line of Credit

Any extension of credit by a financial institution is a line of credit. These all have terms such as interest, maximum amount that can be borrowed, and time limits for repayment.

Loan Fraud

When a borrower intentionally gives false or incorrect information on a loan application, it is considered fraud. This is a criminal offense. Mortgage fraud is investigated by the FBI. All mortgage lending companies are required to send a mortgage fraud warning document from the FBI to all applicants. For more information check out the "white collar crime" section at fbi.gov.

And this one time...

When I began my career in the loan industry I was working with self-employed borrowers. When I requested their tax returns, they said that they had to get them from their CPA. We received the information from their CPA and turned it in to the lender for underwriting. The lender pulled a 4506T (tax transcript). The transcript the lender received back from the IRS did not match the tax return information that the CPA had submitted. The CPA had made a tax return just for the lender to show higher income! The borrowers, as well as their CPA, could have gone to jail for loan fraud. Their loan was denied. This is a big no-no! Lenders are now required to report suspected loan fraud.

Last summer, I was working with borrowers that came to me to purchase a primary residence. However, a lot of the information they were giving me did not add up. They had a 4-bedroom/3-bath house in a nice suburb, valued around $350,000, and they wanted to buy a 1-bedroom condominium with a sales price of $90,000— as their new primary residence. Although one of their children was going away to college, the obvious question of sleeping quarters for their second child came up. This was a red flag to our underwriter that the property would be an investment property instead of a primary residence. When I shared the concerns of the underwriter with the borrowers, they withdrew their loan. Since lenders are now required by law to report suspicious loan activity, I had to fill out a ton of paperwork.

...at mortgage camp...

National Credit Repositories

This is another term for companies that maintain national credit reporting databases. Again, the three main national credit bureaus, also national credit repositories, are Equifax, Experian, and Trans Union.

Notice of Default

This is a legal and formal written notice that a borrower in default will receive from the lender. Legal action may be forthcoming once the Notice of Default has been issued.

⑦

Calculating Income & DTI

This chapter includes information about income and debt-to-income ratios, one of the Four Keys to Mortgage Qualification. Knowing your income and your debt-to-income ratios helps the lender determine your ability to repay the loan. For traditional loans, your income is calculated as what you report to the government, not the cash flow that you take in on an annual or monthly basis. Below I will explain the different ways lenders review your income and then discuss debt-to-income ratios in detail. After reading this chapter you should be able to understand the amount of income that will be used to calculate your repayment ability and also how to calculate your debt-to-income ratios.

Income

Gross Income

In the simplest terms, your gross income is the amount of money you made in a specific tax year. Gross income is listed on your W-2, the form issued by your employer for the purpose of your federal and state taxes. See Box-1 on your W-2; it's labeled "wages, tips, other compensation." You can also find your gross income on your IRS Form 1040; it's Line 7. Some people wonder why the lender needs to see the W-2 if they already have the IRS Form 1040, or vice-versa. The reason your lender needs both your W-2 and Federal Tax Returns is that if you are married, the W-2 income is combined on Line 7 of the joint tax return. The lender needs to know who makes how much income. In addition, you may have tax write-offs that are deducted from your W-2 income.

If you are paid hourly, the lender will calculate your income based on the adjusted gross income of your last two filed tax returns and year-to-date pay stub. If you are a salaried employee, the lender will use your salary minus any tax deductions you write off. If you recently got a raise, the lender will factor that in once you have been receiving the increased pay rate for 30 days. If you just started a new job, the lender will count that income once you have been on that job for 30 days, unless you have gaps in employment. If you have large gaps in employment that are not explained by life circumstances such as pregnancy, moving, medical issues, etc., this could lead to denial of your loan application.

When couples file jointly, the lender will need to see the W-2 forms for each person to make sure the W-2 Box 1 entries match the total of Line 7 on the filed 1040 return. Also, when a person is applying for a loan alone, the lender still needs to compare the gross income on the W-2 to the gross income on the IRS Form 1040. If someone has multiple jobs, the total of all W-2s needs to match the entry on the IRS Form1040. It's all for verification of income.

If you have tax deductions and write off lots of income, be careful and get a pre-approval, not a pre-qualification, to make sure the lender will really lend you what you want or think you can qualify to borrow. It's even more important to get pre-approved if you are self-employed or paid on a 1099 basis. For self-employed borrowers, the lender will take an average of the adjusted gross income of the last two years. However, if your most recent self-employed adjusted gross income shows a decline, the lender will use the most recent annual income instead. There are a few tax deductions that may be added back in, such as depreciation and mortgage interest.

Self-employed borrowers often have a very difficult time closing on a loan, especially if they write off a lot of income with tax breaks. Basically, I see it like this — the government is subsidizing the interest rates. If you don't pay the government income taxes, you're not going to get the government rates.

And this one time...

The Preacher's Payroll Story

I was working with a new client last year that was employed as a preacher. He came to me very upset that the bank he had originally done a mortgage loan application with was not able to help him. I let him know that I would be happy to try to assist him and asked if he knew why they had turned down his loan application.

This is a very sensitive issue for most people and lots of times people don't understand the loan process or why they may not be approved. Turns out that the preacher was not able to prove all his income. Although he worked for several churches and each church paid him, because of tax laws (that's how he explained it to me; I am not a CPA, so I took his word for it), the churches did not report all of the income they paid him to the government. So, he did not have 1099s to prove his income.

If you don't show your income to the government, the lender is not able to use it for loan qualification. We were able to pre-approve the preacher for a loan, but not nearly the loan amount he wanted to buy his new home. He was devastated since he had already written a sales contract with his real estate agent and it had been accepted. This is an example highlighting why you should get pre-approved with us before you go shopping for a home. We save you time, money, and, heartache.

As for the preacher, he was able to cancel the purchase contract since his real estate agent wrote the contract contingent upon financing and he didn't qualify for financing. Because of this contingency, he was able to get his earnest money back. Had he gotten pre-approved prior to shopping for his new home, he would have saved himself much time, trouble, and, heartache.

...at mortgage camp...

Adjusted Gross Income

Very simplified, your gross income less deductions is your adjusted gross income (AGI). On an IRS Form 1040, your AGI is on Line 37. Your adjusted gross income could be higher (depending on other types of additional income) or lower than your gross income; it's usually lower if utilize tax deductions.

Net Worth

The value of all assets less total liabilities, which is often used as an underwriting guideline to indicate credit worthiness and financial strength.

Debt-to-Income Ratio (DTI)

Debt-to-income ratio is a critical component of your loan approval or denial. This information lets the lender know how much you can afford to pay on a monthly basis. So, there are two DTI ratios that underwriters use to compare your monthly income to your monthly debt—the front-end ratio and the back-end ratio. These are also known as the top ratio and bottom ratio, respectively. The front-end debt-to-income ratio is the calculation of your housing expense (soon-to-be-debt via your mortgage) compared to your gross income. The back-end debt-to-income ratio is the calculation of all of your monthly debt (including your new total mortgage payment) compared to your gross income.

The lower your DTI, the better your standing with the lender. If you have a high DTI, there are steps you can take to either lower your debt to not only get approved for a mortgage, but to also put yourself in a better financial position so that owning a home is not a producer of massive financial and emotional stress on a monthly basis. Through DTI, you can see how lenders are looking at more than just whether or not you have collections on your credit report; you are being scored on how much and what types of debt are on your credit, even if you have always paid on time. The rest of this section will help you understand how DTI ratios are calculated so that working towards your mortgage is a step towards your dreams and goals rather than a fear-based monthly scramble.

Calculating Your Debt-to-Income Ratio

Front-End Ratio

The front-end DTI ratio compares just your new monthly mortgage payment (your new debt) to your gross monthly income. For the front-end DTI, with different loans there are different acceptable ratios. First you must know your adjusted gross monthly income. This is your income before taxes. If you do not have a set salary because you are self-employed or commissions are a part of your pay package, ask your lender for help with determining your gross monthly income. As referenced above, sometimes determining income can be tricky. Once you know your adjusted gross monthly income, you will make calculations based on the type of loan you are seeking.

Different loan types have different DTI ratio caps. For an FHA loan, the monthly mortgage payment should be no more than 29% of monthly gross income (before taxes) and the mortgage payment combined with non-housing debts (back-end or bottom DTI, see below) should not exceed 43% of income. For conventional loans, the front DTI should be no more than in the 26-31% range, and, the back-end cannot be more than 43%. For VA loans, the back-end DTI should be no more than 43%. However, there may be exceptions to these guidelines. For example, I have seen loans government with back-end DTI's of over 50% get approved if the borrower has outstanding credit, significant reserves, and/or makes an additional down payment.

These ratios basically inform the lender about your ability to make the payment. The ratios are crazy high numbers anyway since they are based on your adjusted gross monthly income. If you are a W2 employee this is your gross before taxes are taken out. Just remember if you max out your DTI it doesn't leave you much room for unexpected expenses.

Be careful. When I bought my first home the lender told me that I qualified for a much higher payment than I was comfortable with. I was a commission only employee and didn't want to have to worry about paying my bills, so I went with the mortgage payment I was confident that I could pay and then still have fun money left over at the end of the month. Who doesn't want fun money left over at the end of the month? Plus, once you buy your new home, you want to make it yours, which usually includes lots of trips to big box stores. You have no idea how many trashcans you are about to own.

Back-End Ratio
The back-end DTI ratio compares the total of all of your monthly debt payments (credit cards, student loans, car loans, mortgage, real estate taxes, insurance, and any other consumer loans) to your adjusted gross

monthly income. Currently, the federal government mandates that the maximum allowable back-end DTI for conventional loans is 43%. What does that mean? Calculate 43% of your gross income (that's before taxes are taken out)—the number you get is the maximum amount of debt, including your new mortgage, that you are permitted to have on a monthly basis. Your back-end DTI is critical to loan approval. Since the implementation of QM, the government will not buy any loans that exceed 43% DTI when a conventional loan is used. QM stands for Qualified Mortgage; this was enacted in January 2014.

If you have a set salary, calculating the maximum allowable debt is pretty straightforward. You'll multiply your monthly adjusted gross income by .43. Adjusted gross income is your income before taxes; this is usually higher than your take home pay. So, if your monthly adjusted gross income is $5,000, 43% is $2,150. That's your basic starting number. If your gross income is $5,000 per month, you are allowed to have up to $2,150 in monthly debt payments. And remember, that's just the maximum that you are allowed to have, the "scraping by" amount. To reduce financial stress, you should aim to have monthly debt that is much lower than 43% of your gross income.

What monthly debt is counted in calculating DTI? Hmmm, good question. Your monthly debt is calculated as the monthly debt that shows up on your credit report, plus any child support or alimony that you are required to pay each month. Monthly debts that show up on your credit report are things such as the minimum payment on your credit or store card(s), car payment(s), student loan(s), and, mortgage(s). Examples of monthly bills you may have that don't show up on your credit report are your cell phone bill, deposits to your 401K, and, utilities such as electric, cable and Internet. If you don't pay your cell phone or utility bills, then they do show up on your credit report—as collections.

Making Sense of the Jargon

Fixed Expenses
Monthly debts that are the same each month. For example, this can be your car payment, student loan, alimony, child support, etc..

Liabilities
Liabilities are any financial commitments for which you are liable,

including all long-term and short-term debt. This can also be a current or past due liability such as a collection, tax lien, or judgment.

PITI (Principal, Interest, Taxes, and Insurance)

PITI is the acronym for the four key elements of a monthly mortgage payment. The first two, Principal and Interest, go directly towards repaying the loan and the interest on the loan. Next, the T, is the property tax on the home or land for which you have taken the loan. Finally the second I, insurance, if required; this could be homeowners insurance and/or mortgage insurance. The property taxes and insurance portions of your monthly payment are placed into an escrow account; when those fees are due, payment is withdrawn from the escrow account. Your lender will send the property taxes and homeowners insurance annual payments in for you.

Let's break this down a bit more for you. P&I = Principal and Interest. This is the monthly amount you pay towards repaying the loan on your mortgage. So, for example, if you borrow $300,000 that's the total amount of principal you will repay the bank. Then there's the interest… let's say you have a fixed interest rate of 4.5% over a 30-year loan. The interest is what you pay the bank as the cost of using their money (which is really someone else's money, but that's another story). So, on a $300,000 loan the monthly P&I would be $1,520.06; that's $1,125.00 interest and $395.06 for principal, initially.

Principal	$395.06
Interest	$1,125.00
P&I	$1,520.06

The loan is amortized over the 30 years (there are other choices, but this is the most popular), so you will pay mostly interest up front. See the amortization schedule at the end of this chapter.

Then there's your property taxes and homeowners insurance. Monthly property taxes are calculated by taking last year's property taxes and dividing by 12. If your property taxes change, you'll either pay more or receive money back, depending on if the tax is raised or lowered.

But, the calculation based on the previous tax year is what is used to determine your monthly payment.

Let's not forget insurance. There are two types of insurance needed for a mortgage loan. Hazard insurance (generally called homeowners insurance) which protects your home from hazards (see how they got that nifty name?) such as fire (not flood or wind, those are separate), accidents, etc. There is also what's called an HO6 policy, required for condominiums, in addition to the master insurance policy that covers the condo. For much more detailed explanations about insurance, see Chapter 16 — Insurance.

And, let's not forget about PMI—private mortgage insurance. If you didn't put down at least 20% you will have to pay PMI or monthly mortgage insurance. And, if you have a homeowners association or a condo association, that will be included with these numbers to calculate your debt-to-income ratio, but is not usually collected by the lender. You are responsible for paying that on your own. It is determined by your Condo or HOA when it's paid, usually quarterly or semi-annually for HOAs and monthly for condos.

PITI Reserves

A cash amount that a borrower must have on hand after making a down payment and paying all closing costs for the purchase of a home. The principal, interest, taxes, and insurance (PITI) reserves must equal the amount that the borrower would have to pay for PITI for a predefined number of months.

Elysia Stobbe

Sample Amortization Schedule on a $300,000 Loan

Sales Price: $300,000
Down Payment: $0 (also no equity in home at time of purchase)
Interest: 4.5%
Start Date: 1 January 2016
End Date: 1 December 2045
Years: 30
Monthly Payment: $1,520.06
Total Payments: $547,220.12

Total Interest: $247,220.12

Year	Interest	Principal	P-Balance
2016	13,400.99	4,839.68	295,160.32
2017	13,178.66	5,062.01	290,098.31
2018	12,946.11	5,294.56	284,803.74
2019	12,702.88	5,537.79	279,265.95
2020	12,448.47	5,792.20	273,473.75
2021	12,182.38	6,058.29	267,415.46
2022	11,904.06	6,336.61	261,078.85
2023	11,612.96	6,627.71	254,451.14
2024	11,308.48	6,932.19	247,518.95
2025	10,990.02	7,250.65	240,268.30
2026	10,656.93	7,583.74	232,684.56
2027	10,308.53	7,932.14	224,752.42
2028	9,944.13	8,296.54	216,455.88
2029	9,562.99	8,677.68	207,778.20
2030	9,164.34	9,076.33	198,701.86
2031	8,747.37	9,493.30	189,208.57
2032	8,311.25	9,929.42	179,279.15
2033	7,855.10	10,385.57	168,893.57
2034	7,377.98	10,862.69	158,030.89
2035	6,878.95	11,361.72	146,669.17
2036	6,357.00	11,883.67	134,785.50
2037	5,811.07	12,429.61	122,355.89
2038	5,240.05	13,000.62	109,355.27
2039	4,642.81	13,597.87	95,757.41
2040	4,018.12	14,222.55	81,534.86
2041	3,364.74	14,875.93	66,658.93
2042	2,681.34	15,559.33	51,099.60
2043	1,966.55	16,274.12	34,825.48
2044	1,218.92	17,021.75	17,803.73
2045	436.94	17,803.73	0.00
TOTAL	$247,220.12	$300,000.00	

Sample Amortization Schedule on a $240,000 Loan

Sales Price:	$300,000
20% Down Payment:	$60,000 (also $60k equity in home at purchase)
Interest:	4.5%
Start Date:	1 January 2016
End Date:	1 December 2045
Years:	30
Monthly Payment:	$1,216.04
Total Payments:	$437,776.11
Total Interest:	$197,776.10

Year	Interest	Principal	P-Balance
2016	10,720.79	3,871.74	236,128.26
2017	10,542.93	4,049.61	232,078.64
2018	10,356.89	4,235.65	227,842.99
2019	10,162.30	4,430.23	223,412.76
2020	9,958.78	4,633.76	218,779.00
2021	9,745.90	4,846.63	213,932.37
2022	9,523.25	5,069.29	208,863.08
2023	9,290.37	5,302.17	203,560.91
2024	9,046.79	5,545.75	198,015.16
2025	8,792.02	5,800.52	192,214.64
2026	8,525.54	6,066.99	186,147.65
2027	8,246.83	6,345.71	179,801.94
2028	7,955.30	6,637.23	173,164.70
2029	7,650.39	6,942.15	166,222.56
2030	7,331.47	7,261.07	158,961.49
2031	6,997.90	7,594.64	151,366.85
2032	6,649.00	7,943.54	143,423.32
2033	6,284.08	8,308.46	135,114.86
2034	5,902.39	8,690.15	126,424.71
2035	5,503.16	9,089.37	117,335.34
2036	5,085.60	9,506.94	107,828.40
2037	4,648.85	9,943.68	97,884.71
2038	4,192.04	10,400.50	87,484.22
2039	3,714.24	10,878.29	76,605.93
2040	3,214.50	11,378.04	65,227.89
2041	2,691.79	11,900.74	53,327.14
2042	2,145.07	12,447.46	40,879.68
2043	1,573.24	13,019.30	27,860.38
2044	975.14	13,617.40	14,242.98
2045	349.55	14,242.98	0.00
TOTAL	$197,776.10	$240,000.00	

$$\textcircled{8}$$

Covering Your Assets &
Down Payment

The money for down payment, closing costs, and reserves will come from your assets. When applying for a mortgage, your assets are critical to the loan approval process. Without assets and the proper documentation of your assets, you may not qualify for the loan. When you apply for a loan there are few loan programs these days (unlike 2004-2006) that will loan you the full amount of the sales price and cover your closing costs. What does that mean? Well, it means that most likely you will need money for a down payment and the closing costs of your loan. There are a few loan types that do provide 100% financing, VA and USDA. Even with 100% financing, you may still need money for closing costs. In this chapter we will discuss the details about covering your assets and down payment.

To understand the concept of down payment you must also understand loan-to-value. Down payment and loan-to-value have an inverse relationship. For example, if you have a 20% down payment, your loan-to-value will be 80%. If you have a 50% down payment, your loan-to-value will be 50%. If you qualify for a VA or USDA loan to put down 0% down payment, your loan-to-value will be 100%. Make sense? Okay. If not, just email me at info@bestmortgagebook.com.

When you close on your home there are various costs involved. Some costs the seller is responsible for, some costs you, the buyer are responsible to pay. For example, some buyer costs are: appraiser fees, state and county recording fees, daily interest, homeowners association fees, lender fees (see more detail in Chapter 12—Fees).

All of these funds must be sourced and seasoned. What does that mean? When I first got into the mortgage business, I remember sitting at a sales meeting and the team was discussing seasoning. I thought to myself, "what does salt & pepper have to do with loans?" I had no idea. Now I know, and soon you will understand. All of your funds for your loan transaction must be yours or a gift to you. That means that you must document the money is your money. You must be able to show the money in your accounts. You cannot keep a wad of cash underneath your mattress and expect to bring it to the closing table. This is where the seasoning (salt & pepper) comes in. You must also be able to prove that your money has been in your accounts for at least 60 days or two statement cycles. Seasoned refers to the timing that funds have been in your account; if funds were just deposited to your account, the funds have not been "seasoned" in the account. If funds aren't seasoned, you must show from where the funds originated; showing where funds have come from is called sourcing the funds. If the lender tells you that your funds must be sourced, that means that you must provide written documentation.

Assets

Assets are your money in various forms. Assets can be cash you have in the bank, not cash under your mattress. So, your checking and savings accounts are examples of assets. Other examples of assets are a money market account, stocks and bonds, 401K accounts, IRAs, your car, life insurance policy, equity in your home, or vacation homes. Things like cars, boats, jewelry, and art are assets, but these types of assets are not used to calculate your mortgage borrowing power or your ability to pay for the down payment and closing costs.

Only liquid assets can be used for down payment and closing costs. For example, although a life insurance policy is considered an asset, unless you can get cash out of it right now, you cannot use it for the purposes of down payment and closing costs. Along these same lines, unless you sell your car and get cash for it (and document in writing), it cannot be used for closing costs.

During the application process, your assets will need to be provided. Don't expect to call a lender and tell them your credit score and that you want 100% financing and they will say, "Awesome, we have a loan for you!" If you hear that, run. Run far, far away from that lender because you are hearing what you would like to hear instead of the reality of the loan qualification process. Even if you do qualify for 100% financing, you will probably need cash for closing costs and reserves. So, be prepared to tell and show your lender how much you have in assets and what type of assets they are— checking, 401K, gift, etc.

During the underwriting process your assets will be examined. Yes, the underwriter will want to see written proof that your money is your money. For loan approval, you will need to provide proof that you have enough money for down payment and closing costs and possibly reserves BEFORE your loan will be approved. You cannot just say that you have the money and show up at the closing table with the funds needed for closing. You will have to prove it to your lender.

The way that your assets are calculated can affect your loan approval. By this, I mean the money you need to qualify with your lender. For example, you may have $10,000 in a 401K, but the lender will use 60% of that as liquid assets (assets you can use now, real cash). Any retirement monies are calculated at 60% because a 40% penalty for withdrawal is assumed. If you have a $10,000 limit on your credit card, don't think you can take a cash advance on your credit card and use that money for down payment, reserves or closing costs. Money on a credit card is classified as borrowed funds; borrowed funds are not an acceptable source of down payment, closing costs, or reserves.

The primary points to remember about assets are show as much as possible, and, don't move assets. You may not need a fat stack of assets to get the mortgage, but the more you can show the lender for loan approval, the better. Also, do NOT move your money around. This can turn into a paperwork nightmare for you and your lender. For example, if you keep $5.00 balance in one account and $10,000 in another bank account and move money back and forth you will need to provide statements to the lender to prove that the money coming in and out of your accounts is really your money in order to use the money from both accounts. It's much easier for you to not move the money around and provide the bank statement with the $10,000 in it.

Down Payment

Down payment is also called equity in the property. Equity is the inverse of loan-to-value. For example, if you have a 20% down payment (equity) 100% - 20% = 80%. Your loan-to-value is 80%—

meaning that your loan compared to the value of the house is 80%. The lender will take the lower of either the appraised value or the sales price to calculate your loan-to-value. For example, if your sales price is $300,000 a 20% down payment would be $60,000. $300,000 x 20%=$60,000. That means that your loan-to-value is 80%.

Your loan plus your down payment must equal either the sales price or the appraised value, whichever is lower. Using the same $300,000 sales price, you would multiply $300,000 x 80%, which equals $240,000. $240,000 + $60,000 = $300,000. I use the 20% number because you must put down at least 20% for most loans if you do not want to have mortgage insurance.

It gets tricky if your appraisal comes in lower than the sales price and your real estate agent is not able to negotiate a lower sales price that is equal to the appraised value. If your appraised value comes in at $295,000 and the sales price is $300,000, then you must put an extra $5,000 down to make up the difference. Ouch! Hopefully your real estate agent will be able to negotiate the sales price down to the appraised value so you can keep that $5,000 in your pocket (never your pocket, this is just a phrase – remember all funds for down payment and closing costs must be sourced and seasoned). If your real estate agent cannot negotiate the sales price down to the appraised value, hopefully an appraisal contingency was written in your contract that will allow you the option to exit the transaction and keep your earnest money deposit. Keep in mind that you do not get a refund for the appraisal, as that work was completed; but, isn't it better to spend $450 for the appraisal instead of losing $5,000 by assuming the sales price was equal to the value of the home?

Note that equity is not always equal to the down payment amount. If your appraised value comes in higher than the sales price, it's to your advantage, and your equity in the property will be greater than your down payment. Let's say your appraisal comes in at $305,000 and your sales price is $300,000; the lender will still use $300,000 for the value. You just get to walk in the door with $5,000 equity in your new home. Congratulations!

FHA, VA, and USDA loans require funding fees. Funding fees are up-front fees that are paid to the government for funding a loan for you. Funding fees may be paid in cash or added to your loan amount. The funding fee makes it a little more complex to calculate the equity from your down payment. Let's say you are using an FHA loan for a $300,000 home; a 3.5% down payment ($10,500) means that your loan amount will be $289,500. With no funding fee, that would mean that your equity in the property is $10,500 on closing day. But, you will have to pay a funding fee. You'll have the option to either pay your funding fee in cash or add it to your loan amount. The funding fee, currently 1.75%, is $5,066.25. Most people choose to add the funding fee to their loan. This means that the $289,500 becomes the 'base loan amount' and the total loan amount is now $294,566.25. Since the total loan amount changed, the equity changes, too. Assuming the sales price and appraisal were equal, now the equity is $5,433.75.

Home Price	$300,000.00
Down Payment	$10,500.00
Base Loan Amount	$289,500.00
Equity in the Property	$10,500.00
Home Price	$300,000.00
Down Payment	$10,500.00
Base Loan Amount	$289,500.00
Funding Fee	$5,066.25
Total Loan Amount	$294,566.25
Equity in the Property	$5,433.75

Making Sense of the Jargon

Deposit/Earnest Money

The deposit or earnest money is a payment towards securing a sales contract on a house that you want to buy. The deposit shows the seller of the home that you are serious about buying the home and paves the way for the seller to take your offer seriously. If the seller accepts your offer, your deposit becomes part of your down payment or funds for closing on the home. Your deposit is returned if the seller rejects your offer. If you change your mind about buying the home, you lose your deposit money. But, when you make an offer, there is a contingency period. During this contingency period you can get your deposit back from the seller if the 'contingencies' you list in your sales contract are not met.

Contingencies can be a satisfactory home inspection or title of the property. Another contingency could be financing approval or appraised value. It's important to know exactly what your contingencies are as well as the timelines for each. They may not all be the same. It's very important that you, your lender, and your real estate agent are all on the same page and working together to meet those deadlines so that your deposit is not in jeopardy. It's also a really good idea to discuss the timelines and contingencies with your real estate agent and lender before you submit your offer to the seller to make sure they are reasonable for all parties. The deposit you submit with your sales contract is also called a binder in some states. It's called a binder because it "binds" your offer to the sales contract once it is accepted. Once your offer is accepted, in some states you're are now "in escrow" because a neutral (usually) third party holds your deposit "in escrow" once your offer is accepted and you have a legally binding agreement.

Down Payment

This is the amount of money you pay in cash towards the purchase of your new home. This money could include money that has been gifted to you from a family member; gifting is allowed for some loan types, but not all. Be sure to talk with your licensed mortgage professional about documenting gifts and how much of your own funds may be required in addition to a gift. The amount of gift allowed, and who may give it to you, varies by loan type. Your down payment plus your loan amount must equal the sales price of the home you are buying. (Note that if you use a loan that requires a funding fee, your total loan amount plus your down payment may be higher than the sales price).

Your down payment and closing costs must be sourced and seasoned. What do fresh ingredients and spices have to do with your loan? It has nothing to do with cooking and everything to do with where your money comes from…you cannot pull $20,000 out of a shoebox and bring it to closing thinking you are going to use that for your down payment. All funds in your transaction must be sourced and seasoned— you must be able to prove where the money came from, the source. Even your deposit binder must be sourced and seasoned. If your wife is not on the loan, she cannot write the deposit check from her account. If so, you will have to document that as a gift and that requires at least 3 additional documents besides a copy of your canceled deposit check. Sound like lots of paper? It is lots of paper.

Source of Funds

Source of funds is the trail showing where your money comes from. Which one of your accounts are you making a payment from? Is the money a gift from your parents? Is it a loan against your 401K? Not from underneath your mattress—that is NOT allowed. The lenders consider un-sourced funds a loan and will calculate that amount with a 5% interest rate IF they allow you to proceed. Sound complicated? It is.

Do NOT move around monies from account to account if possible, as you will have to provide documentation to prove that it is your money. This will create even more paperwork. Your lender will usually require your last two bank statements for all asset accounts where your down payment (if needed) and closing costs are coming from. If you have multiple accounts and move your money around, you will have to provide all the account documentation to prove it is your money. If you know you are planning to buy your dream home in the next 60-90 days and you don't like extra paperwork, just move your down payment and any estimated closing costs into one account and let it sit there.

Earnest Money (Deposit)
This is also called a binder or "in escrow" in some states. It's called a binder because it "binds" your offer to the sales contract once it is accepted. It's called in escrow in some states because a neutral (usually) 3rd party holds your deposit "in escrow" once your offer is accepted and you have a legally binding agreement.

9

Property—Your New Home

Property type can affect the type of loan you are able to get for your mortgage. Are you looking for a single-family home, or a condo? Will your new property be your primary residence, a second home, an investment property? If a specific loan type is more important to you than property type, speak to your licensed mortgage professional during the pre-approval process to find out what type of properties you should look at when you begin your home search. Below I will discuss some of the more common property types and conditions that could affect the availability of loan choices.

Property Types

Single Family Residence (SFR)

A single family residence is a freestanding home. This can be in a planned unit development (PUD), in a subdivision, in a city, in the suburbs, or, in the country. An SFR qualifies for all types of mortgage financing. Sometimes if an SFR is on a large plot of land, such as a farm, special financing may be required. Usually SFRs are the easiest type of property for which to get a mortgage.

Remember, if you choose a home in a PUD, a deed-restricted community, a covenant community, or any other type of community that requires membership in an association, you must abide by the rules governing the community. In some cases this may mean a required monthly or annual fee, also known as dues. Governed communities also may have rules about what you can do to your yard, your home, even how often you must mow your lawn; some are more strict than others.

If there are community dues required for the home, these dues are factored into your monthly payment (see PITI in the Jargon section of Chapter 7). That means the dues are also factored into the calculations for your DTI ratios (Chapter 7). A very important thing to remember is that though these fees are factored into your monthly payment, you do not pay them as a part of your monthly mortgage payment. The lender will list these community/association fees (you must disclose these) on your loan application, BUT, the lender does not pay these fees out of your mortgage payment—you are responsible for paying these fees on your own, in addition to your monthly mortgage payments. Typically, association fees are not escrowed.

Townhouses

A townhouse is a single-family home that is attached to your neighbor's home on one or more sides. As far as mortgages are concerned, townhouses are generally treated like SFRs. So, it's usually easier to get a mortgage on a townhouse than it is to get a mortgage for a condo.

With townhouses, you will need to be cognizant that needed repairs adjacent or attached to your neighbor's property may be done jointly, so choose your neighbors wisely! Townhouses often require community association fees just like the PUD fees listed above under single-family residences. In some cities, townhouses are called 'row houses.'

Friends of mine who live in a row house have columns on the front of their house; these columns are shared with the row homes to each side. The columns needed to be replaced just as regular maintenance due to normal wear and tear over time. Fortunately they were friendly with one of the neighbors; this neighbor chose to share in repair costs for the shared column. But, the neighbor to the other side refused to share the cost of repairing the shared column on that side. So, my friends were stuck paying all of the costs associated with repairs to that shared column.

Condominiums

Condominiums (condos) come in many forms, such as large apartment-style buildings, adjacent townhouse style, or even freestanding buildings such as duplexes or triplexes. Condos have the most restrictions as far as mortgages are concerned. For example, if the condo master insurance policy doesn't have enough coverage for the lender, your loan will not be approved. Or, if the condo association is in the middle of a lawsuit or parts of the general areas of the condo are damaged, the lender may not approve your loan. Another scenario— if the reserves for the condo association budget are not satisfactory, the lender may not approve your loan. Finally, if 15% or more of the owners in the condo community are behind in their condo dues, the lender may not approve your loan. These factors have nothing to do with you or your creditworthiness, but are significant factors in your loan approval or denial. Don't take this personally. The lender is trying to protect your investment as well as reduce the investment risk taken by the lender.

Under the bi-laws that govern condos, the property outside your walls is shared by all of the condo owners. This can include your front door, your patio or balcony, parking space, trees, lawns, sidewalks, pools, tennis courts, and community rooms or buildings. This does not necessarily mean you have access to everyone's parking space or balcony. It does mean that you have a shared financial responsibility for the maintenance and upkeep of the shared space. This is typically included in your monthly condo fee, as is the cost of the master insurance policy for the condo community.

Unexpected surprises, such as a new roof, that have not been pre-planned in the budget can be assessed to all of the condo owners. That means that each owner is responsible to pay the assessment so that the repair can be done. Assessments can be as low as a few hundred dollars and as high as tens of thousands of dollars. If you do not pay the assessment, a lien can be put against your property by the condo association. The condo association can also put a lien against your property if you do not keep current with your regular monthly condo fees.

As a condominium owner you own from the walls into your unit, often called "walls in." This means that you own your drywall, your flooring, everything attached to the inner walls, cabinets, bathroom fixtures and showers and tubs, appliances, and, of course, all of your personal treasures. Sometimes this can be confusing. For example, let's say your sink is stopped up. If it's stopped up because you did not clean hair out of the drain, repairs are your responsibility. If the sink is stopped up because of a blockage in the main sewer drain of the building, repairs are the responsibility of the condo association.

A condominium has a condominium association that governs everything you do, just like a PUD. In some cases, you may only be able to paint your front door certain colors! Or your patio may only be a certain size or material. It's very important to read your condo association regulations BEFORE you buy so you know what rules you will be required to follow.

Condo communities also require payment of monthly condo association dues, just like a PUD. These dues are factored into your monthly payment (in the PITI, see PITI in the Jargon section of Chapter 7). That means the dues are also factored into the calculations for your DTI ratios (Chapter 7). A very important thing to remember is that though these fees are factored into your monthly payment, you do not pay them as a part of your monthly mortgage payment. The lender will list these condo association fees (you must disclose these) on your loan application, BUT, the lender does not pay these fees out of your mortgage payment—you are responsible for paying these fees on your own, in addition to your monthly mortgage payments. Typically, condo fees are not escrowed.

And this one time...

I recently helped a client purchase a condo. It was her first experience as a homebuyer. She was so thrilled to be moving into her first home. She bought a cute condo in an historic part of town. After she had closed on her new home, about 3 weeks later, she received a bill from the condo association. The bill was for her monthly condo fees. In the loan documents (on her application and at closing) she had seen the condo fee included in her monthly payment, so she assumed it was being paid with her mortgage. When she received the bill from the condo association, she was livid! She thought she was being ripped off and paying her condo fee twice!

I don't blame her for being upset. I would have been, too, if I had to pay my monthly condo fee twice. But, that wasn't the case... she was not paying twice. All the mortgage documents show the total monthly obligation so that the borrower doesn't have any surprises at closing. It's important that borrowers understand what comprises their total monthly obligation. So, although at the closing table the condo fees were listed as part of her total monthly obligation, she is responsible to pay that portion of her monthly obligation to the condo association directly through monthly billing. So, just remember that you will pay your condo or association fees in addition to paying your monthly mortgage bill.

...at mortgage camp...

Cooperative (Co-op)

Co-ops are the ultimate condo. Co-ops are truly collectively owned by all of the owners in the building. When you buy a co-op unit, you become an owner-partner in the cooperative corporation that owns the entire structure. If you get a mortgage to buy a co-op unit, you are responsible for that mortgage, and also for paying a part of the collective/cooperative mortgage on the entire structure (if applicable). For mortgage purposes the minimum documents that will be reviewed by the mortgage underwriter are the co-op budget, the co-op profit and loss statements, the co-op balance sheet, and the co-op by-laws. Not all lenders will finance co-ops. In addition, the co-op board has to vote you in for you to be eligible to purchase a unit in the co-op.

Duplexes, Triplexes & Quads

Generally, multiple-family homes are treated as investment properties unless you are going to live in one of the units. If it's an investment property, it may be eligible for conventional financing (see more below). If you are going to live in one of the units, it may be eligible for VA or FHA financing. Mortgages for these types of properties are a bit more complex, so be sure to ask your licensed mortgage professional about additional guidelines and costs associated with such properties. If the building has more than four units, it is considered commercial property, not residential property, so you would have to get a commercial mortgage. That's a can of worms not opened in this book!

Land

This may seem like one of the easiest mortgages to get because there is no home to be inspected or roof that may need repairs. After all, it's just land, right? However, from a residential mortgage perspective, land is a riskier investment because not everyone wants land; if the lender gets stuck with land because the borrower defaults, it's usually much harder to sell to recoup the lost money. Land mortgages, also called 'lot loans,' have much stricter credit and reserve requirements. Typically land also requires a minimum of 20% to 30% down payment.

Usually for lot loans the loan term is much shorter. For example, the typical lot loan may have a 10- or 15-year amortization schedule with a 3-year balloon. This means that your payments may be amortized over 10 or 15 years, but the note is due in full in 3 years. This means that if you paid the scheduled amount of the monthly mortgage payment it would take you 10 or 15 years to pay of the entire loan amount, but you actually only have 3 years to pay off the entire loan amount. So, either you make the scheduled payments and then pay a large sum at the end of 3 years, or you make much larger payments. Or, at the end of 3 years you can refinance the lot loan—if you are eligible. Or, you might be able to get a construction-to-perm (permanent) loan to build a home on the land. Then, once construction is complete, you can apply for one of the other mortgage products, such as a government loan or a conventional loan. If you have enough equity at that time, you can pay off the lot loan with part of your new mortgage.

Primary Residence

Primary residence, also called owner-occupied, means it will be your only home and/or you will reside in it most of the time. After initial purchase, the expectation is that you will live in this property for at least one year. A primary residence has the least restrictions and qualifies for almost all types of loan financing. In addition, primary residences have the best interest rates. Primary residences have the least restrictions on down payment requirements. For VA and USDA loans, the minimum down payment is zero—thank you veterans. For FHA loans, the minimum down payment is currently 3.5%. For conventional loans, the minimum down payment is currently 5%, unless you are a first time homebuyer, then it is only 3%.

Second Home

A larger down payment is required for second homes. Currently it is 10% for conventional financing. When you are buying a home, second homes are not eligible for VA, FHA or USDA loans (government mortgages). All of those loan types are for primary residences only.

However, another benefit of FHA & VA loans if you are no longer living in the home is that you may still refinance those loan types as non-owner occupied. You may be able to refinance to a lower interest rate even if you no longer live in the home. You will be subject to a slight increase over an owner occupied refinance versus a non-owner occupied interest rate, but you may still refinance if you meet the other loan qualifications.

Investment Property

Also called non-owner occupied, investment property is sometimes bought for the benefit of a family member but is usually purchased for real estate investment purposes. This means that you do not intend to live in the home, not even on a part-time basis. Investment properties are eligible for conventional loans only. Investment property requires the highest down payment; the minimum down payment is currently 20%.

Property Value

The value of the property is important in your loan transaction. The value must appraise for at least the sales price in your sales contract. This affects your loan-to-value as well as the down payment for your loan.

Property Condition

The condition of your property is very important. It must be habitable. What does that mean? Certain loan types have different requirements, but generally speaking it must be move-in ready. So, the heat must be working and the power must be working and in safe condition. The roof can't be leaking. The deck can't have a big hole that you could fall through to get injured. You may be able qualify for a home renovation loan to fund repairs for these items, but that's an entirely different book. Just think—do I want to be my own general contractor? Do I want to live in a construction zone for months? If you do, then ask me about those loan types (info@bestmortgagebook.com). Otherwise, it's a good general rule to stay away from those types of properties.

Some repairs, such as a new roof, can be taken care of by the seller prior to loan closing. (You'll need a hazardous roof replaced so you can get insurance on your home). However, some sellers may not have the money to make the repairs. Sometimes repairs can be done after closing. The lender may allow you to escrow for repairs. For example, I recently worked with an investor to help him purchase his 5th rental property. The seller, Fannie Mae, refused to do any repairs to the home. Since the sales contract was an AS-IS contract, Fannie Mae was in a position to decline any negotiations for repairs. The appraiser noted two items that required repair for the home to be classified as habitable: the floor in the living room, which had unsafe gaping holes, and, the tile in the bathroom. We were able to escrow for these repairs and close the loan for our client.

However, I worked with a borrower earlier this year for which we were not able to escrow for repairs. The appraisal and sales contract noted that the septic tank needed to be replaced. Since a septic tank not working properly would be a major impediment to a habitable new home, this item had to be replaced by the seller prior to closing the loan. Contact your lender before you write an offer on a home to find out if any needed repairs may be escrowed for at closing. But, the more you can avoid this, the better (unless you are a construction professional). You will encounter enough stress on moving day without having to coordinate major repairs, too. Take it easy on yourself!

Making Sense of the Jargon

Acre
An acre can be measured in any shape. An acre is measured as 43,560 square feet.

Appreciation
Appreciation is the increase in value of your home over time. One way the government keeps track of this (for tax purposes) is through annual property appraisals. If you want to compare the government assessment of your property value to the market, you can hire an appraiser or check out your property on Zillow.com.

As-is Condition
For our purposes, as-is can refer to the type of sales contract or the value of a property in an appraisal. For sales contract purposes, this means that the property is being sold as-is, which means the seller is not required to do any repairs before closing. It is your responsibility to get a home inspection to determine the condition of the property. If major repairs are needed, this cannot be negotiated into the sales contract. Be careful writing a sales contract on an as-is home; you may lose your deposit if you back out of the contract if you fail to comply with the terms of the contract.

Assessor/Property Appraiser
An official appraiser is a government employee, usually within the county department responsible for tax assessment. The appraiser is responsible for determining property values for the purpose of assessing taxes.

Assessed Valuation

Assessed valuation of your property as determined by the government body that assesses tax on your property.

Building Code

Building codes are the minimum requirements for structures and the systems within structures or on the property. Building code regulations are issued and enforceable by state and local governments. Examples of building codes include HVAC, electrical, plumbing, outbuildings, septic, and roofing.

Covenants

Covenants are the legally enforceable rules that govern planned unit developments, covenant communities, and deed restricted communities. Covenants are transferred to the new owner when the property deed transfers.

Deed

The deed is the legal document that defines ownership of property. The deed is transferred when ownership changes from one person or entity to another. Deed information is publicly recorded and contains a legal description of the property and the owner/s. The deed is also known as the title.

Deed-in-Lieu

It's actually a deed in lieu of foreclosure. This gives you and the lender a better option than foreclosure. It means that you give the title of the home back to the lender, and then the lender releases you from the debt and sells the home to recover your unpaid mortgage debt. It's better than foreclosure because it saves the borrower and the lender both time and money that would be spent in court under a foreclosure. It also reflects differently on a borrower's credit than a foreclosure would.

Depreciation

Depreciation means that your property has declined in value. One way the government keeps track of this (for tax purposes) is through annual property appraisals. If you want to compare the government assessment of your property value to the market, you can hire an appraiser or check out your property on Zillow.com.

Easements
Easements allow someone other than the owner of the property to legally access the property. Easements are defined in the property deed and recorded on the survey of the property. Some examples of easements are space for public fire hydrants, city electrical boxes, alleys, and common driveways. Easements may affect property value.

Eminent Domain
Eminent domain allows the government to take privately owned property for public use. The government is only required to pay fair market value to the property owner.

Encroachments
An encroachment is a structure that crosses the legal bounds of a property, onto the legal bounds of another property.

Encumbrance
An encumbrance is anything that affects the property deed/title. Examples of encumbrances include liens, loans, leases, easements, and covenants.

Fixture
A fixture is anything permanently attached to the property, such as a deck or porch. Fixtures can also be in the home. Examples of interior fixtures include ceiling fans, fireplace mantles, and lighting.

Home Inspection
See Chapter 18—How to Choose a Home Inspector.

HVAC
HVAC is the acronym for Heating, Ventilation and Air Conditioning; a home's heating and cooling system.

Property (Fixture and Non-Fixture)
For real estate transactions, property is the collateral for the loan. Property is the land within the legally described boundaries noted on the deed and all permanent structures and fixtures.

Raw Land
Unimproved land.

Setback
Setback is the legally defined space requirement between the property line and a structure or between the property line and a public space

such as a road or alley. Setback may also be the required space between structures on adjacent properties.

Survey
This is the diagram of your property that defines legal boundaries, easements, encroachments, rights of way, improvement locations, buildings, fences, pools, etc. Some lenders require a survey and/or survey endorsements to confirm that the property and all features or easements are recorded correctly on the deed.

Variance
A variance is an exemption from the zoning law that allows the property to be used for purposes not defined in the existing zoning law applicable to the property.

Zoning
Zoning defines the legally allowable uses of property, as dictated by local governments. Some examples of zoning include residential; various types of commercial, such as retail or industrial; and, mixed use.

(10)

4 Stages of the Loan Process

Origination, Processing, Underwriting, & Closing

The loan process moves along in four stages: origination, processing, underwriting, and, closing. During this process, all of your documents are reviewed; the underwriter will compare your submitted documents to the underwriting guidelines to determine if you qualify for a mortgage—to borrow a very large sum of money. If you qualify for the loan, the underwriting process will then produce a list of requirements you must meet to get the loan. Underwriting is the part of the loan process during which a designated professional reviews the loan guidelines and compares those guidelines to the information supplied by you and the processor.

Knowing the players involved in your loan process, and what their responsibilities and limitations are, will give you an advantage throughout the process. One of the major time setbacks comes from mortgage applicants not meeting paperwork deadlines for the processors and underwriters. Because most people that apply for a mortgage are not mortgage experts, it's understandable that the inner-workings of the process is a mystery for them. But, understanding just a little can help you take ownership of the process and make sure that you are fulfilling all of your responsibilities as an applicant.

In our digital-focused world with an insta-app for everything, it's easy to want to believe that we can just say we want a loan and have someone else search through digital records for an accounting of our monetary history. Luckily, we still have privacy, and the mortgage experts will need you to get many of the documents for them. Sometimes the requests may be annoying — you're busy, too!

If you know these requests are coming, you'll be prepared — expect them and be ready to meet the requests to speed along your mortgage process. The end goal is closing day and getting the keys to your new home! Keep your perspective that you're asking someone to help you get a home by fronting you the money to pay for it. In the big picture, the paperwork and document requests require a small amount of time compared to the many years you will be enjoying your home. The main people on your lender's team involved with your loan, from the point that you apply to closing day, are the loan officer, loan processor, the underwriter, and, the closer.

1. Loan Officer & Origination

A loan officer is (hopefully, depending on who you are working with!) a licensed individual with the National Mortgage Licensing System. The loan officer is like the quarterback for your loan. Your loan officer is the main coordinator between processing, underwriting and you, the client. He or she lets you know what loan programs you qualify for and can educate you on the pros and cons of each. A licensed loan offer goes through rigorous screenings such as an FBI criminal background check, a credit check, hours of technical and ethical education and testing to obtain this license. In addition your loan officer is required to take continuing education and screenings annually to maintain their license. However, the requirements are different based on the type of financial institution where the loan officer is employed, so ask your loan officer about their license, education and experience. You can verify that your loan officer is licensed and that their license is current at nmlsconsumeraccess.org

The licensed loan officer is the only one who can legally lock the interest rate for your loan and discuss the details of the terms of your loan with you. The loan officer is responsible for originating your loan (starting your loan file), and, sending to you and discussing with you your loan disclosures, which include the terms and closing costs associated with your loan. The loan officer should be skilled in the various loan programs that her/his lending institution has to offer and should be adept at discussing the nuances and explaining them to you. Your loan officer should be willing to take the time needed to explain this in detail to you and answer any questions you may have about your loan options and the loan process. If not, get a different loan officer or shop for different lending institution immediately as this is critical for the largest purchase of your entire life. Email my team at info@bestmortgagebook.com for help and use our Checklist: Questions to Ask When Interviewing a Lender at the end of Chapter 4.

The best loan officer that you can find is going to care about how your loan choices affect you personally. Although many people imagine finance-related professions to be somewhat dry, there are loan officers out there that care deeply about helping their clients. These loan officers have a professional commitment to excellence and an emotional investment in humanity—they want to see you not only get a home, but to also know that they have helped you get a mortgage that is financially sound for your specific situation.

Origination is the start of your loan. The loan officer takes your loan application, pulls your credit and reviews it, reviews your income, assets, and sales contract against their loan guidelines, and, sends your loan disclosures to you. Loan disclosures include your 1003 (loan application), Good Faith Estimate (not to be confused with an Itemized Fee Worksheet, but more on GFE vs. Itemized Fee Worksheet later), Truth in Lending (TIL), and a host of other documents depending on what loan type you have applied for. Yes, I said "applied for" as opposed to "getting". Keep in mind that there are no guarantees for loan approval. Loan guidelines can change at any time without notice. So, it's very important that you choose a lender that has a proven track record— a proven track record of closing on time and closing loans. According to Fannie Mae, of loans originated, less than 50% actually close. That's scary! Our branch closing ratio at the time of writing is 95% of loans originated and locked. That means that our closing success ratio is well over 200% above the national average.

2. Loan Processor & Processing

A loan processor should be your cheerleader. Along with your loan officer, he or she is the direct conduit to the underwriter; the underwriter decides the fate of your loan. The processor is often the unsung hero. He or she works tirelessly on your behalf, with little appreciation. Processors are in the office, so they rarely get to meet with you (the client) and get to know how awesome you are; nor are processors released from their relentless tasks that keep them at their desks, so they can't attend the celebration of the closing and rejoice with you.

The processor orders and reviews your appraisal, title work, verification of employment, verification of deposits (bank statements, 401K, checking/saving accounts, money market, gifts, etc.), debt-to-income ratio, and, cash-to-close — just to name a few of the many loan requirements that are needed to send your loan to the underwriter for review (and hopefully approval!).

Once you have accepted (signed) your loan disclosures and sent the lender all your income and asset documentation, your loan file moves to processing. The processor reviews the documentation you have provided for accuracy (compares it to your loan application which is form 1003) and the loan qualification guidelines. The processor will also order your appraisal, title work, verification(s) of employment, review your assets, loan disclosures, and, submit your loan to underwriting.

3. Underwriter & Underwriting

The underwriter reviews your credit, income, and asset information, as well as your property, title, and appraisal in comparison to the loan underwriting guidelines. The underwriter is the referee for your loan. She/he does have some flexibility to make decisions that may be critical to your loan. You will rarely have direct access to the underwriter working on your loan. Your loan officer and processor usually communicate with the underwriter directly, on your behalf. The underwriter is responsible for giving the final approval on your loan so that you can go to the closing table and get your keys.

Underwriting reviews the documentation for your income, assets, reserves, debt-to-income ratio, credit score and credit report, liabilities, as well as the title work and appraisal for the property you are buying. The loan originator, loan processor, or underwriter runs an automated underwriting program. This is called Desktop Underwriter (DU) for Fannie Mae loans, Loan Prospector (LP) for Freddie Mac loans and Guaranteed Underwriting System (GUS) for USDA Loans. VA Loans can be automated using LP or DU. Each of the loan programs produces underwriting findings.

If the findings are rated Approve/Eligible (DU or GUS) or Accept (LP), the underwriter then reviews those findings for accuracy and compares them to the information submitted with the loan. Then the underwriter approves or adds conditions (questions and requirements) to each point on the findings. From start to finish, a loan can have upwards of 100 conditions. Luckily most of these are taken care of for you by other people on your team: the appraiser, title company, loan processor, loan originator, credit intermediary, mortgage loan funder, title company closer or notary, real estate agents, or, other professionals involved with your loan or home purchase.

However, most likely you will also be asked to supply additional paperwork such as updated pay stubs, a divorce decree (if applicable), proof of funds, marriage certificate (if applicable), updated bank statements, and proof of withdrawal. Expect to supply lots of paperwork to begin your loan process, as well as during your loan process. If your lender didn't need it, they wouldn't ask for it. If you expect this and know it's coming, it will help make your loan process smoother than if you fight it. Appraisal and title may have conditions that provoke more conditions as well. For example, if the home you want to purchase does not have clear title, that will have to be cleared prior to closing. This is more common in today's market since there are so many foreclosed homes.

The bottom line is that all of the conditions of the loan must be met in order for your loan to close. Be aware that some conditions will open other conditions. For example, if you are asked to supply updated bank statements, be aware that the processor and underwriter will review those bank statements. If you have large deposits, you will be asked to provide proof (source) of where those deposits came from. So, don't just send in bank statements and think you are done. This is where lots of confusion and frustration come into play when people don't expect it and don't understand the necessity.

And this one time...

Lisa's Cousin Marly's Tips to the Bank

I have had a few clients that get tips as part of their compensation. If you are in the gambling business this is usually strictly controlled and clearly noted on paychecks. When tip income is clear on paychecks and

W2s or 1099s, it helps make the loan process go smoothly. However, if you are in the food service industry, like Marly, large bank deposits of tips suddenly need to be explained when you're getting a mortgage.

If you receive tips and your employer does not note the tips on your paycheck, you must claim them on your tax returns to the U.S. Government if you want to be able to use that income to qualify for a mortgage. Marly had a surprise with another lender who made her write letters of explanation for all her tip deposits. Seems obvious since she gets tips, but since they were not documented on her pay stub she had to write an explanation for every single cash deposit resulting from her cash tips.

So, the lesson here is that the income earned, and deposited to the bank, from cash tips was not a problem— the lender just needed the applicant to fill out extra, unexpected paperwork and attest to the fact the source of the money deposited was legally earned. If you're making regular deposits of legally earned money, the lender can expect that you will continue to earn that income. If you are making deposits of mystery money, how could the lender consider that regular income to count towards or against your risk factor as a borrower? If you earn and deposit income from cash tips, just be prepared for questions and a little extra paperwork.

...at mortgage camp...

Underwriting Guidelines

There are a lot of rules and regulations in the mortgage industry. These rules protect both the borrower and the lender. The loan process is a combination of legal requirements, guidelines of government and financial institutions (such as Fannie Mae and Freddie Mac), and the guidelines imposed by the lender to which you are applying for a loan.

Automated Underwriting

In automated underwriting, the loan officer, processor or underwriter runs your loan through a computer program. These automated underwriting programs can be specific to loan types and loan standards of large lending entities. So, your lender may require that your loan conforms to the standards of another financial institution, such as

Fannie Mae. Using the automated underwriting program ensures that all guidelines and requirements are met. Much of the paperwork that your lender asks you for comes from the requirements of the automated underwriting program.

4. Closing

Closing is the end goal (Yippee!!) and final part of the loan process. Keep in mind that all conditions of your loan must be satisfied in order for your loan to proceed to closing. If you are bringing money to the closing table, you will need to bring certified funds from accounts you provided and that were verified on your loan application. Certified funds can be a wire or cashier's check. Make sure you have the amount of funds needed to close and how it must be sent to closing. You can get this information from your lender or the title company.

Once all of your loan conditions are satisfied, your loan proceeds to closing and quality control (QC). QC is a final review of all of the loan documents. At a minimum this includes your credit and income documents, title and appraisal paperwork. The Closing Department is the division of the lender's team that prepares your loan closing documents and sends them to the title company. Closing documents include detailed instructions to the title company on how to prepare your HUD-1 Settlement Statement. The title company prepares the HUD-1 and sends it to the lender for approval. Once it is approved by your lender (sometimes this may take a few revisions back and forth between the lender and the title company), the lender sends all the rest of your closing documents to the title company for you to sign at closing. These documents may vary slightly by lender and loan type, but include at least your HUD-1, loan application, and, all disclosures.

It's All Coming Together...
Why does the loan officer, processor, underwriter and closer matter to you? When choosing your lender, you want to talk to as many of these people as possible to understand who the people are that will be working on something very personal for you—your new home and the future of your financial commitment in the form of a major loan. These are the people who will be working to get you to the closing table— you want to know that they care about getting you there smoothly and quickly. Are they polite? Do they care about you as a person or are you just another loan in their pipeline? How many other loans are

they working on? What is their success ratio? Can you count on them? Do you have direct access to your loan officer and loan processor? For more important information critical to your closing success, see the Checklist: Questions to Ask When Interviewing a Lender at the end of Chapter 4.

Usually a home mortgage is the biggest purchase most people make in their lifetime, yet they forget to consider being very choosy about who is on their team. There's much more to choosing a lender than just the interest rate. Think about picking a team for a neighborhood flag football game. You want strong players, but you also want players that want to be on your team, that care about winning, and care about having a good time with each other during the game. Your team is critical to your success and to your desired outcome of actually going to closing, rather than the unexpected game-over of finding out underwriting will not approve your loan after you have already spent money on an appraisal, home inspection, and other costs. Understand the game, know your players—you'll set yourself up for success.

Making Sense of the Jargon

Compensating Factors
Compensating factors are additional factors that may be considered by the underwriter, such as low payment shock, good history with non-traditional tradelines (such as utility and car insurance payments), rent, and possibly employment of others living in your household.

Direct Endorsement (DE)
Direct endorsement is when a lending institution is certified by the FHA to underwrite loans in-house instead of submitting them to FHA for an underwriting decision.

(11)

Documents

Documents can make or break your loan. With documents, the devil is in the details. You will submit your asset accounts (checking & saving accounts, money market, IRA, CD, 401K, 403B, brokerage accounts, etc.)—any accounts you plan to draw money from for your down payment and closing costs. Supplying the proper documentation in the correct form can save you days of frustration and loss of time. The clock starts ticking when you sign a sales contract and everyone is working hard to get you to closing; so, if you do not respond quickly to document requests, you are not only risking your mortgage and your binder, you are also making it very difficult for the lender to finalize full approval for your loan. Also, if you cut corners and do not send documents in the proper form, you are burning time. Sending incorrect documentation can burn up several days—a day for the request, another day sending incorrect documents, another day the lender has to request correct documents…and so on.

If you want to be a proactive participant in your loan process, pay attention to what is requested and what you send. Failure to provide the correct documentation for loan approval will stop the loan process. If you are not able to provide the requested documentation for the underwriter, sorry to say, you will not be approved for the loan. I was working with a client last year that sent a scanned copy of his wife's driver's license that was illegible. After months of requesting a clear and legible copy of the driver's license, we finally received a clear copy and were able to move forward. Thank goodness! Something as simple as taking a picture of your driver's license with your smart phone and emailing it to your lender is a silly thing to hold up your loan closing.

Be prepared to get lots of documents and you will save yourself time and mental anguish. I once had a client that was wondering why his loan was not closing quickly. We had asked the borrower again and again for the documents, but he just said he couldn't find them. Unfortunately, as much as I despise paperwork, if the underwriter needs it to approve your loan, you must provide it. If you need help with the document format or where to find some documents, just ask your lender. They should be happy to help you. If not, consider another lender.

Many of the documents you are asked to supply, such as a driver's license or photo ID, are required by law. If you have questions about the document requests—wonderful!— I can't preach enough about staying informed. Just make sure to ask your questions right away to keep the momentum going towards full approval and a fast closing. As you'll see in more stories below, just a little attention can save tons of time and contribute to the smoothest loan process possible. Although everyone is working for you via the fees you pay them, they are also human beings working to get you a lump sum of money that you would not have otherwise. Keep in mind that all of these people want your loan to be approved and they have the best intentions in being your advocate for loan approval.

Un-Altered Documents

When asked to send documents to your lender, it is extremely important that the documents are in their original form and have not been altered. The most obvious reason that documents must be in original form is fraud prevention. Mortgage fraud is punishable by the FBI. Employees at the lending company could go to jail for accepting altered documentation from you. Also, the lender must approve your loan in accordance with a multitude of regulations, laws and requirements, many of which pertain to verification of all information. If you send altered documentation, you put the lender at legal risk for not diligently verifying your information. For example, I had a client send bank statements and she had whited out the account number on all of the pages. The account number is critical to matching and sourcing deposits to verify her income, savings, and payments. This client's loan process was put on hold until she submitted unaltered bank statements.

Send Complete Documents

When you are asked to send documents, you need to send all pages. If asked for your tax return, don't just send the first two pages (unless you use the 1040EZ form and that's all you have). If you have child credits, write-offs, donations, or own a business (you will need to send those returns too), your tax return will be longer than two pages. It's also important to send all pages from the beginning. If you send a partial document upon the request, you're setting yourself up for potential challenges later in the loan process. The missing pages may have information that changes the calculation of your income. If your income (and debt-to-income calculations) changes, your conditional loan approval will probably change, too. That's a big surprise late in the game. No one wants those surprises. Not you, nor your loan team.

Asset statements are another example highlighting the importance of sending all pages. Even that last page of your checking account that you may use to balance your account is critical. The underwriter must see all pages of the document because it cannot be assumed that the missing information is irrelevant. For example, the last page that may be meaningless to you could include a bank loan that doesn't show up on your credit report. That loan is required to be counted in your debt-to-income ratio. If you send pages 1-5 of a 6-page bank statement, and page 6 includes a loan, that's another surprise you don't want later in the process.

Don't Send Screen Shots
Be sure you are sending actual statements. In today's world of online banking, it's easy to think you can just send a screen shot of your bank balance or financial transactions and that will suffice. How will the underwriter know it's yours if it doesn't have your name on it? It's just like in high school, put your name on your paper. The document needs to be an official, full statement (last 60 days is usually the minimum required) on the financial institution's letterhead that includes your full name, account number, and, mailing address. When I receive a screen shot with a client's nickname on it and his or her checking balance, I usually say that while I may assume it's your money since you sent it to me, the underwriter is tasked to prove that it is actually your money when used for down payment, closing costs, and, reserves. This is the reality of the loan guidelines and requirements for approval.

Sending a screen shot of your bank statement and not the actual statement slows down the entire loan process. For example, once your loan is underwritten your loan officer and processor will be working on gathering the conditions for your full loan approval. If one of those conditions is to source your funds and you've sent a screen shot of your bank account, not the actual bank statement, the entire process is on hold. The bank statements are a condition of your loan and are required for the underwriting process. Though you may have turned in all other documentation and conditions, your loan package cannot be sent to underwriting until ALL critical documentation requirements and conditions are met. Why? Because assets are a critical piece of the approval and many other conditions can be tied to it. This applies to other critical documents too, such as pay stubs, your earnest money deposit, and income tax returns, to name a few.

Send Current Documents & Keep the Process Moving

Another important tip regarding documents is to keep in mind that they expire. Yes, expire. Everything in your loan file needs to be current. So, if the loan process is stalled, new documents may be requested. For example, spring is one of the busiest times of the year for home purchases. What else happens in the spring? Tax time! If you have been conditionally approved based on your last two years of filed Federal Tax returns and you just filed a new one, guess what? The oldest one is no longer used by underwriting and underwriting must use the new one to update your income. If you show a huge loss on your most recent tax return, your loan approval may be in jeopardy! Life is always changing, so, the sooner you can get to closing the better! It leaves less time for unwanted surprises. Ask your licensed loan officer what timing may affect your loan approval and interest rate during your process.

Q&A Session

Q: What tips do you have about providing documents for a faster loan process?

Elysia: Be sure to have your documents ready to go to your lender at the time of loan application. Include all pages of every document your lender has requested. No missing pages, no pages that are cut off or partially obscured will be accepted, you have to send legible copies. See our list of documents at the end of this chapter. Once you are in the loan process provide your lender with exactly what they asked for (no more, no less) within 48 hours of the lender's request. Drawing it out will only put your loan and earnest money deposit in jeopardy.

Q: What document issues can slow down the process or even make a person lose the mortgage?

Elysia: Moving around money. Putting money in your account that is not yours or that you are not able to show a paper trail where it came from. Buying a new car, mattress, or, furniture. All the things you will want to get for your new home. Do NOT buy them before you close on your new home or you may not have a new home. New debt is added to your debt-to-income ratio, if you buy a new car, it may disqualify you for the loan.

Q: How can people use document knowledge to their advantage?

Elysia: The more prepared you are with your documents, the easier it is for the lender and YOU.

Q: What other things do documents affect— for example, a house a person can choose?

Elysia: If you go car shopping it drops your credit score about 50-75 points. This will have a snowball affect on your documentation. Do NOT do that before you apply for a loan. You will have to supply additional documentation about the new loan showing the loan amount and monthly payment. The new loan may affect your debt to income ratio, which may affect what loan type and property type you can qualify to purchase. In addition, the new loan may influence your credit score which can affect what type of property you can buy as well as down payment requirements and type of loan. If you must buy a car, do it after your loan has closed. Feel free to check with your lender BEFORE you buy ANYTHING. You can check your credit at annualcreditreport.com.

Q: Can documents affect closing?

Elysia: Yes, if you do not provide the correct documents that your lender has requested, your loan will not proceed to closing.

Q: Is there anything else documents may affect— credit? closing? points? loan type?

Elysia: Yes, there are lots of documents that must be submitted by someone other than you that can affect loan approval and loan type. Such documents include title work, condo questionnaires, and, co-op documents.

And this one time...

Asset Documents – Wanita, my former colleague

On the other hand, if you are applying for a traditional mortgage, you must supply your asset statements for several reasons. You must show that you have a down payment (if needed for your loan), cash to close, and reserves. Do not white out your account #'s. I was working with a former colleague from back in my radio days and when she sent me her bank account statements, she whited out all the account #'s.

What a waste of her time. She then had to reprint all the documents and resend them. This was back in the days before scanners. Bummer for her, more time gone, a delay in getting loan approval. The lender needs to match up the account numbers from month to month and make sure it's your money.

If you're not sure about exactly what is required, just ask! A good rule of thumb is not to alter documents. Seems kind of basic, but you'd be surprised how this is a major problem for lenders. This has to do with fraud as well. If you don't trust your lender, then get a different lender. If you're just paranoid, that's another story. Seek professional help. I'm not qualified to go near that issue!

...at mortgage camp...

Checklist: Documents Required for Loan Application

❑ Last two pay stubs

❑ Last two month asset account statements (checking, saving, IRA, 401K, 403B, Roth IRA and/or 401K, brokerage account (stocks/bonds, etc) anywhere your down payment and closing costs are coming from

❑ Last two W2s or 1099 depending on how you are paid

❑ Last two years of filed & signed Federal Tax Returns

❑ If you are self-employed you will be asked to provide your business tax returns, too

❑ Last two W2s or 1099s, depending on how you are paid

❑ Copy of your Driver's License and Social Security Card
(Patriot Act to prove your identity as well as prevent loan fraud)

The income and asset requirements are a series of twos. I don't make up the mortgage guidelines and requirements, but I can tell you why I think it's a series of twos… For starters, your lender is required by the government to review your income and asset documentation. But, there's a pattern of stability they are looking for in the documents. Let's say you made $100,000 two years ago and all of a sudden you double your income; the lender is probably going to average your current income with your past income so that you don't go bonkers and buy more than you can afford.

The lender is looking for a pattern of saving, paying your bills on time, and not bouncing checks (don't worry, if your pattern isn't perfect you may still qualify). The lender may also look at payment shock. What's payment shock? It's when your current rent is less than half of your new estimated mortgage payment. If you've been paying $1,800 for rent and your new mortgage is $4,000, are you going to be able to consistently budget and make that payment? Good question! There is a method to the madness of getting approved for a loan.

Checklist: Document DON'TS

❑ DON'T send illegible documents that are blurry, cut off or too dark or too light to read!

❑ DON'T send screen shots of your bank account statements!

❑ DON'T send just page one or just the summary page — send all pages of all requested documents!

❑ DON'T white out or black out account numbers!

❑ DON'T white out or black out your social security number on your W2s, tax returns, and pay stubs!

❑ DON'T send three months of statements if you are asked for two months of statements. Always send exactly what is requested!

❑ DON'T pack any documents in your moving truck or storage unit— even if you think you're done with them. Keep all documents you have submitted or might need to submit handy right up until you sign at closing!

❑ DON'T waste time being annoyed about document requests; just send the documents quickly to keep your loan process on track! Stay focused on the positive!

Checklist: Documents Required for Loan Processing

❑ Last two years filed/signed Federal Tax Returns (all pages of personal, and, if applicable, business, too)

❑ Last two years W2s or 1099s

❑ Last two months asset accounts (all pages of all accounts)

❑ Copies of Driver's License & Social Security Card (this is for the Patriot Act)

❑ Contact information for landlord

❑ Contact information for your homeowners insurance company

❑ Copy of your fully executed (signed by all parties) sales contract

❑ Copy of marriage certificate or divorce decree if applicable

❑ Copy of your bankruptcy or foreclosure if applicable

In addition, if you currently own a home you will also be asked to supply the following:

❑ Current mortgage statement for all properties owned

❑ Current property tax statement for all properties owned

❑ Current homeowners insurance declarations and invoice for all properties owned

❑ Copy of listing of your current home for rent or sale or copy of executed HUD if already sold

Checklist: Documents Required During Processing & Underwriting

❑ Most recent pay stubs

❑ Most recent asset accounts (all pages of all accounts)

❑ Sales Contract addendums (if changes occurred since the original executed copy was supplied)

❑ Clear WDO/pest for VA Loans

❑ Signed updated loan disclosures, such as lock confirmation and proof of appraisal receipt

❑ Copy of your earnest money (binder) check clearing your bank

❑ Signed gift letter, proof of donor's ability to gift, and, proof of funds being transferred to your account (if gift is applicable)

❑ Letters of explanation

Checklist: Documents Required for Closing

❑ Two legal forms of ID, at least one must have your picture on it

❑ Certified funds for amount due at closing—ask your lender and/ or title company if a certified check or wire is preferred. Keep in mind you will have to show where these funds are coming from with updated asset statements and proof of the transfer of funds or gift.

❑ Driver's License: This is required by the Patriot Act; lenders MUST ask you for this and you MUST provide it in order to proceed with the loan process. If your lender cannot read the information on your DL, you will be required to send a clearer picture. Thank goodness, do you want someone else taking out a loan in your name? No, that's called identity theft.

For more information about the USA Patriot Act, search for "USA Patriot" on the U.S. Department of Justice website at justice.gov

The best thing you can do with all documents is provide clear, readable copies of everything your lender requests. There is no sense in arguing, this will only make you frustrated. The lender is not asking you for additional documents because they need paper for a bonfire. They are asking because it is required for your loan. Also, if you are asked for documents, it is YOUR responsibility to get the documents to your lender. If not, you are holding up the loan process and this is NOT good when you have a $5,000 or $10,000 earnest money deposit check on the line.

Please keep in mind these checklists are the basics of what is required, your lender may ask you for more documents depending on the information you supply. Also, if you already gave your Driver's License and Social Security Card, W2s and signed Tax Returns to your lender at the time of loan application you should not have to supply again them during the loan process unless something has updated or changed with your loan. You will need to bring your Driver's license to closing, no exception there and that's for your own protection. Providing updated pay stubs and asset account information is standard as part of the loan process, so be prepared.

Making Sense of the Jargon

Annual Mortgagor Statement

This is the annual statement you will receive from your lender; the statement outlines how much principal remains to be paid on your loan and how much has been paid towards interest and taxes. Your annual interest you have paid on your loan is sent to you by your lender, on an IRS form called a 1098. You may be able to use that as a tax deduction. Be sure to consult your licensed tax professional.

Application

The first step in the official loan approval process; this form is used to record important information about the potential borrower necessary to the underwriting process. Be prepared to answer lots of questions, and, once pre-qualified, giving the lender everything—including your first born. Okay, just kidding! But it's a ton of paperwork. The loan application is also called form 1003.

Document Recording
After closing on a loan, certain documents are filed and made public record. Discharges for the prior mortgage holder are filed first. Then the deed is filed with the new owner's and mortgage company's names.

Good Faith Estimate
An estimate of all closing fees including pre-paid and escrow items as well as lender charges; must be given to the borrower within three days after submission of a loan application. Also called a GFE.

HUD1 Statement
The HUD-1 Settlement Statement is also called the "closing statement" or "settlement statement." This is a complete itemization of all closing costs, yours as well as the sellers. This shows who is paid what and how much. All fees involved with your loan purchase are on it. Don't gloss over it, read it, review it with your lender and ask questions. Items you will see on the HUD-1 include real estate commissions, title fees, loan fees, county government fees and escrow amounts.

Lien
A lien is an encumbrance on the title and must be satisfied in order to transfer ownership of the property. It is a claim of money against the property. Examples of liens are a tax lien, mechanic's lien, or, a bank lien. A lien release, and the original lien, is recorded with local government.

Lien Waiver
A lien waiver is a legal document used to protect the homeowner from other entities that may try to file a lien on their home. For example, you may request a lien waiver from a contractor to prevent subcontractors from trying to file a lien against the homeowner if there is a dispute between the contractor and subcontractor.

Notary Public
A notary public is a public official that has the legal authority to verify and certify the authenticity of signatures on legal documents. A notary public will stamp the documents with an official seal upon witnessing the document signing.

$$\textbf{\large (12)}$$

Fees

Fees? Who wants to know about fees? All you want is to get into the house, right? Who cares what it costs? Believe it or not, there are lots of people I work with that don't want to discuss their closing costs in detail. I have not figured out if this is because they are too busy with other important things (kids, moving, work, life, yoga to de-stress, etc.) or because they just chalk all of the costs up to a necessary evil.

Actually, I would guess that the plethora of numbers is a bit daunting to normal humans who only do this once or twice in a lifetime. Us mortgage geeks are familiar with them as a daily occurrence, just like a dentist is familiar with gore and the powers of numbing medication when pulling a tooth. Unlike when those dentists ask you questions while their hands are in your mouth and you're rendered unable to answer, you can and should talk to your lender during the entire mortgage process. Ask questions! This is your loan commitment and you are paying fees for everyone involved to work for you.

You should always review your numbers with your lender. It may not change a whole lot, but you will know what's what. By the way, you won't write a check (for closing costs). These must be given to the title company via certified funds; that means you must bring a cashier's check or wire the funds. Also, if the numbers change at closing, you will want to know what changed and why. Whether your seller is helping you with closing costs or not, it's money, usually lots of money. Keep in mind that buying a house is usually the largest purchase you will make in your entire life. Don't you want to know what it really costs?

Q&A Session

Q: Why are there so many fees?

Elysia: There are lots of fees because buying real estate is very complex and involves lots of entities, such as your lender (a team of professional specialists and many hours of work to get your loan approved and to the closing table), the appraiser (yes, s/he is a separate entity and doesn't work directly for the lender), title company (they have a processor, underwriter, and closer, too!), the state and local governments, and finally, the real estate agents—your real estate agent and the seller's real estate agent get paid by the seller, not you, but those are still fees.

Those are the big ones, the most common fees you will encounter during the mortgage process. Sometimes there are other parties that get paid at closing, such as homeowner or condominium associations. If you are buying a home or unit governed by an association, your membership in the association is a condition of purchase. The associations receive a fee for confirming the amount that the current owner owes the association (if any) and transferring paperwork from the old owner to you.

The entities that get paid on the HUD-1 are: real estate agents, lender, appraiser, title company, state & local governments (recording & taxes), homeowners insurance, homeowners/condo association, home inspector and surveyor. There may be others, but these are the main players you will usually see on the HUD-1.

Q: How does fee payment affect the application process?

Elysia: If your lender charges you an application fee, you must pay that to get either pre-qualified or pre-approved, or, you must pay at the time of loan origination (when the lender actually starts working on your loan). Next, you must pay for the appraisal of the home you want to buy before the appraisal can be ordered. Most sales contracts have a 10-day allowance for home inspection and appraisal. This means you must order both right away. Once ordered, both are dependent on the licensed specialists' schedules, and, sometimes on the listing agent's schedule, as well. The listing agent needs to let the home inspector and appraiser into the house for the inspections. They usually work on a first come, first serve basis and coordinate with the real estate agent from there.

As far as the appraisal process is concerned, some lenders and AMSs (appraisal management services) have a collateral review process they must go through before the appraisal is approved. Since the home you want to purchase is the collateral for your mortgage, appraisal companies have an underwriter, as well. That's the "collateral review process" that is performed by the appraisal company. That review process may request changes and/or revisions from the appraiser, and that may also take up more time. VA Loan Guarantee currently allows their appraisers 10 business days to complete the appraisal, and then the VA has to approve it. Once approved, the VA issues a Notice of Value.

Q: How does fee payment affect getting to an on-time closing?

Elysia: It shouldn't affect closing on-time as long as you pay for your appraisal and home inspections when requested to do so. Home inspections and appraisals are usually paid well before closing, in the first 10 days of the sales contract. Most fees are paid on the HUD-1 at closing.

Q: What is the HUD-1?

Elysia: The HUD-1 is your settlement statement. That is the final document with all the dollar amounts that pertain to you buying your new home. You will read more about the HUD-1 in Chapter 20.

Q: What fees are typically paid by the buyer?

Elysia: Who pays which fees is outlined in your sales contract. This varies by state for title fees and state fees, and also depends on whether or not your real estate agent has negotiated seller help. Some fee payments can be negotiated for you by your real estate agent. Some fees depend on whether you are buying new construction or an existing home. These fees can also vary with the loan type. For example, with a VA loan, the buyer cannot pay a closing fee to the title company or pay for a pest inspection (even though it is required for the loan). Typically the seller will pay those fees. Be sure to ask your lender how much seller help is allowed with your loan program.

You should ask your lender and your real estate agent which fees are usually paid by the seller in the state where you are buying the home. You should also ask the lender and real estate agent what fees the seller may be required to pay.

Ask your real estate agent which fees are usually negotiable and which are not negotiable. Be reasonable with your expectations and negotiations. You are dealing with other human beings. Emotions and stress may be running high on your side or on theirs. Believe it or not, most real estate deals fall apart over differences as little as $2,500. That may sound like a big number, but if you're talking about a $300,000 loan, it's less than 1% of the loan.

Q: What fees are typically paid by the seller?

Elysia: This varies by state for title fees and state fees. It also depends on if the real estate agent has negotiated seller help. It can also vary with the loan type. When you ask your real estate agent and lender which fees you are supposed to pay (see above), also ask them to specifically list which fees the seller must pay or could be negotiated for the seller to pay.

Q: Should any fees be paid by the mortgage banker or the real estate agents?

Elysia: The lender and the real estate agents do not pay fees associated with your home purchase. All fees associated with the real estate transaction and the mortgage are paid for by the consumer(s) initiating the transaction, the seller and buyer.

The mortgage banker may incur costs with a credit re-score or update, but it is the client's responsibility to pay for such costs. A credit re-score can be done for the borrower by the lender. For example, let's say a borrower has a collection on her/his credit report that s/he was unaware of until it showed up on her/his credit when s/he went to get the mortgage. The lender may require that the collection be paid off in full before closing the loan, and, this information must be documented by a credit intermediary, which is a third party. That third party doesn't work for free, so the lender may charge you to update your credit so that it meets underwriting guidelines. This is much better than a loan denial!

Sometimes a lender may choose to give the borrower a lender credit. For example, some lenders have an on-time closing guarantee. Don't worry, there are strict timelines you will have to meet in order for the lender to be able to help deliver their guarantee. It's a team effort. If the lender doesn't meet the closing date and it's the lender's fault, they may credit you the cost of the appraisal for example. There are circumstances that may allow the lender to give a credit to help with the borrower's closing costs; but, beware; this comes with a higher interest rate. Just remember, it's a trade-off—you pay for the lender credit through the higher interest rate. Be sure to work the numbers before accepting a credit in exchange for a higher rate.

Q: Are there any fees that should be paid by anyone else?

Elysia: The seller pays the commission for both real estate agents. This is usually 6 percent—3 percent for each agent. Every once in a while there is an exception, but this is the general rule.

Q: What fees often come as a surprise to the buyer?

Elysia: Home Owners Association (HOA) estoppel fee. This is a fee that the buyer pays to the HOA usually through the title company to confirm that the seller of the property is current on their financial obligations for the homeowners association. If they are not current, the seller must be brought current (pay for) with any outstanding dues and fees before or at closing in order for the property to transfer ownership. You may be able to negotiate if the buyer or the seller pays this fee. You can see this fee or fees on the HUD-1 Settlement Statement at closing.

Condo questionnaire fees also usually come as a surprise. This questionnaire is filled out by the condo association management company and is reviewed by the lender to make sure the condo meets the lender's guidelines for condo property approval. It's typically 10-30 questions, depending on the type of condo review, and can cost anywhere from $75 to $350. The cost of the questionnaire is determined by the condo association, not the lender. The buyer is responsible for paying this fee.

Q: What tips do you have for buyers regarding fees?

Elysia: Ask what the fee is for and is it required. For example, state fees are required. A survey may not be required if an acceptable survey is already provided. But you may want to get a new survey. This is why you want to ask questions.

Q: What fees could home-buyers ask someone else to pay?

Elysia: For VA loans, the seller may pay all the closing costs; however, there is a cap of 4% on concessions. Also, the lender may only charge a maximum of 1% origination and a 1% discount fee. For the full, most up-to-date list, ask your lender.

So, if you are getting a VA loan and your real estate agent can negotiate for all your closing costs to be paid for by the seller, the likelihood that you can get into your new home with zero cash out-of-pocket is pretty good! Keep in mind—this must be negotiated by your real estate agent, in writing in the sales contract, or it doesn't exist. No handshakes or oral agreements will do; this is a legally binding contract you are entering into, and everything in writing counts.

For USDA and Conventional loans, the seller is currently only allowed to pay up to 3% of the buyer's closing costs. FHA loans allow the seller to pay up to 6% of the buyer's closing costs. This must be negotiated up front by your real estate agent and must be included in your sales contract, or it won't exist.

Q: What fees do buyers get duped into paying?

Elysia: There are two to look out for…One—application fees over $100. Take advantage of the time spent during the application process and ask as many questions as you want. Make sure you are comfortable with the answers you get. If not, ask more questions. Be informed and be empowered—this is your purchase and your commitment.

Two—look out for lock fees. If you are paying to lock your interest rate—beware. This is a fee you pay upfront, whether you close on the loan or not. If you are asked to pay a lock fee, it is usually non-refundable. If you are asked to pay a lock fee, you want to make sure that your loan is already conditionally approved and you are aware of and comfortable with all of the loan conditions. What if you are not able to meet one of the conditions and the lender cannot close your loan? Is that lock fee refundable? Usually not. Also, don't confuse a lock fee with an origination or discount fee.

Q: What fee warning stories do you have?

Elysia: The government has over-regulated the mortgage industry. What started out to protect the buyer from "junk" fees has actually created more administration work for the lender. This gets passed on to the borrower in some shape or form.

One time a borrower came to me after obtaining a good faith estimate (GFE) from another lender. He had been loyal to that lender for his previous purchase transaction. The lender was taking advantage of him and charging two points—one discount point and one origination point.. his loan amount was $250,000. One 1% is $2,500. That's $5,000 he was being charged by the other lender. We were able to match their interest rate with no points and save them $5,000!

Q&A Session: Questions from Past Clients

Clients: We're looking at the Truth in Lending form. This shows amount financed is $579, 861.00... why not $584K. The $584 loan amount is listed on the "Residential Loan Application"... shouldn't the number on these two forms match? As we discussed previously we want to ensure we are avoiding PMI.

Elysia: The amount financed is not supposed to match the amount on the loan amount. The amount financed on the Truth In Lending has to do with financing. This number is derived from the loan amount minus the Pre-paid Finance Charges of $4,139.00. (Loan amount of $584,000-Pre-paid finance charges of $4,139.00= Amount financed $579,861.00). The amount of your loan on page 1 of the loan application is $584,000 and is the actual amount you will be borrowing (and responsible to repay per the amortization schedule).

Clients: We're looking at the Continuation Sheet/Residential Loan Application. There's a page that talks about "your charges for other settlement services" box 6... required services that you can shop for..." do we need to list the "home inspection" fee that we already paid for? Are we required to have a survey done? If we want to do this... do we go through you?

Elysia: Home inspection is not a required service, so you don't need to list it. It is recommended, but not "required" which is why it's not on the list. You can choose your survey company; we do not order it for you. Usually the title company or your real estate agent will assist you with this.

Clients: We're looking at the Truth in Lending form. The Flood insurance box is not checked. I thought you said previously that had to be included in Virginia. If it is required, are we required to buy it as part of this package or can we buy it on our own and pay it directly?

Elysia: At this time, it is not known if Flood Insurance is required for your loan; that is why the box is not checked. A Flood Certificate is pulled during your loan process. If it is determined that Flood Insurance is required for your loan, then you can choose the homeowners insurance company you want to use for Flood Insurance (as well as your hazard insurance, which is required). If Flood Insurance is not required for your loan, you can choose that option if you want and it does not need to be escrowed with us.

Clients: We're looking at the PMI Disclosure Sheet. Why does this form say that we are acquiring a mortgage that requires PMI? I thought we were able to avoid PMI?

Elysia: That is a standard disclaimer, so you know when it is required. Should the appraisal come in lower than your sales price, PMI may be required. As your loan is structured currently, as long as the appraisal comes in at value, you should not need PMI.

Clients: Sorry for all of the questions.

Elysia: It's my pleasure to answer the questions so you feel comfortable!

Making Sense of the Jargon

Application Fee
This is a one-time fee paid to the lender when applying for a loan. The amount varies by lender.

Appraisal Fee
The loan applicant is responsible for paying the appraisal fee. The loan applicant gives the lender the money for the appraisal fee and then the lender gives it to the appraisal company or the loan applicant can pay the appraisal management company directly. The loan applicant should not pay the appraiser directly. This fee can vary by the type of loan and the size of the loan. For example, the VA appraisal fee is regulated by the VA and varies by state. An appraisal for a conventional loan may be less expensive than an FHA appraisal. If your sales price and/or loan amount are over the conforming limits, the appraisal fee may be higher.

Appraisal fees are dictated by the appraisal type, but can vary by the lender since the lender selects the appraisal management companies. The lender is no longer allowed to order the appraisal directly from the appraisal company. The lender must order appraisals through an independent third party, an appraisal management service. This requirement is new, enacted after the mortgage meltdown. In 2007 the HVCC Home Valuation Code of Conduct was introduced and in 2010 Appraiser Independence was introduced.

Closing Costs

This is the big enchilada if your seller isn't covering some or all of the closing costs for you. Closing costs are all the fees included on the HUD-1 Settlement Statement for final property transfer not included in the price of the property. Although closing costs vary by state, you will pay several entities at the closing table. Thankfully, the seller usually pays your real estate agent and their own real estate agent. Yippee!

You are responsible for paying the lender, the title company, the state, and any costs associated with or incurred by those entities. What does that mean? Well, if the lender processed your loan, you will be charged for the work they did. If the lender ordered an appraisal and your credit report on your behalf since it is required for the loan, those are fees that you are responsible for and they are associated with the closing of your loan. The title company may order a survey of the property, as well as a title search. You will be responsible for paying both of those fees.

See why this is a complicated process? Holy cow! We joke in our industry that getting a loan to closing is like herding cats. Have you ever tied to walk a cat, let alone heard a group of them? There are several different entities with various timelines, experience, industry knowledge, and commitment. Once your loan is originated, about 20 people will be involved in the process. What you want is 20 people who understand they are on the same team working diligently to ensure that they succeed in getting you to your dream of home ownership. You want the real estate agent, the lender, the appraisal company, and, the title company to all work together.

You also want the lender's team to work together. A good question to ask your lender is how many people are on their team? How often are they in communication with their processor? Their underwriters? How often can you expect an update? We update our clients at least weekly on the progress of their loan. We also touch base once or twice a week on any loan conditions that we need from the borrower. See our checklist at the end of Chapter 4-Questions to Ask When Selecting a Lender.

Typical closing costs include charges for the mortgage loan such as origination fees, discount points, appraisal fee, survey, title insurance, legal fees, real estate professional fees, prepayment of taxes and insurance, and real estate transfer taxes. A common estimate of a buyer's closing costs is 2 to 4 percent of the final purchase price of the home. A common estimate for seller's closing costs is 3 to 9 percent. See the Closing Costs Checklist at the end of Chapter 20.

Discount Fee and Discount Point

A discount fee is what you pay to reduce your loan interest rate. Typically one discount point will buy your loan down a quarter of a point in interest rate. A discount point on your loan is one percent of the total loan amount. So, if you have a $300,000 loan, one discount point is $3,000. Let's say your interest rate with zero discount points is 4.5%. Your monthly principal and interest payment would be $1,520.06. If you spend one discount point, $3,000, to buy down to 4.25% interest rate, then your monthly principal and interest payment would be $1,475.82. The monthly savings from buying down the interest rate would be $44.24. This is an annual savings of $530.88. This means that it would take a little under 6 years to break even on the $3,000 spent for the discount rate.

So, if you think this is your forever home, it might be worth considering buying down your rate. Discount points can be applied to any type of loan— a fixed rate loan, adjustable rate loan, FHA loan, Conventional loan, USDA loan, or, VA loan. It's an easy calculation that your lender should be happy to do if you ask her/him. With interest rates so low right now, buying down the interest rate is not as common as in the past.

Funding Fee

This is the upfront fee, paid at closing, that is required for government loans. For more information, see Chapter 13.

Home Inspection Fee

A home inspection is a detailed and thorough examination of the structure and mechanical systems of the property to determine quality, as well as soundness and safety. The purpose of a home inspection is to inform the potential homebuyer of any repairs that may be needed. The homebuyer generally pays inspection fees. In addition to the basic home inspection, there are additional inspections that you may choose to have, such as a pest inspection or a 4-point inspection. Home inspections have come a long way—now they have thermal imaging, moisture detection equipment, and lots of other technical innovations to find hidden issues. A home inspection is not the same as a home appraisal.

Loan Origination Fee

An origination fee is what you pay as a cost of the lender originating (starting, opening) your loan file. This fee may or may not be inclusive of processing, admin, and, credit report fees. Though the origination fee may be required to start your loan, you actually do not pay the origination fee until closing day.

Points

A point is equal to one percent of the principal amount of your mortgage. A point can be applied as a loan origination point or a discount point. Points are charged by lenders in both fixed-rate and adjustable-rate loans in order to cover costs and/or buy down the interest rate. Depending on how your sales contract is written, these points may be paid for by the buyer or seller and are paid at closing.

Pre-paids

Pre-paids are fees collected on your HUD-1 Settlement Statement at closing that are for future bills associated with your home. This generally includes homeowners insurance, escrow accrual for homeowners insurance and taxes, daily interest to the end of the month, and, Funding Fees or PMI (Private Mortgage Insurance), if necessary. Read more about PMI in Chapter 16.

Pre-payment

Pre-payment is when you pay off a portion or all of the loan balance before the scheduled due date.

Pre-payment Privilege

This is the right of the borrower to prepay on any portion of the principal of the loan. Some loans may not allow pre-payment without paying a fee. Ask your licensed loan officer whether your loan has a prepayment privilege or a prepayment penalty!

Pre-payment Penalty

A clause in some loans (usually adjustable rate mortgages) that allows the lender to charge a fee to a borrower for paying off a loan before it is due. This can apply to you if you choose a partial payment of principal or to repay the entire loan within a certain time period. A partial payment is generally defined as an amount exceeding 20% of the original principal balance.

This type of penalty is usually added to loans when the lender offers to pay your closing costs. Nothing is for free—there is a catch sooner or later. The penalty is also usually added to ARMs. Prepayment penalties are usually in force for two to three years from closing. There are also different types of prepayment penalties. One type of prepayment penalty is applied if you try to sell or refinance your home within a short time period, usually 2-3 years.

There are also different types of pre-payment penalty periods. A hard prepayment penalty is applied when your current loan is satisfied (paid in full). If you win the lottery and want to pay off your loan, if you have a hard prepayment penalty you would have to pay the penalty fee to completely pay off your mortgage. Prepayment penalties are important to keep in mind if you are not sure how long you will be in your current home.

If you have a soft prepayment penalty, that usually only kicks in if you refinance your loan (not if you sell your home). For example, if your current interest rate is 5% and you have an opportunity to refinance to a 4.5% mortgage, you will pay the soft prepayment penalty. Also, if your loan only has a soft penalty and not a hard penalty and you sell your home after a short time, you will not have a prepayment penalty. If you decide to move for personal reasons or take a new job, you are not going to be happy to pay that prepayment penalty to sell your house. The amount of penalty is usually a percentage of your loan and the details are outlined in your note or mortgage.

Premium
Premium is the amount paid on a regular schedule, usually annually, to maintain insurance.

Private Mortgage Insurance (PMI)
PMI is insurance that is paid for by the borrower to protect the borrower's lender if the borrower defaults. The lender selects the PMI company for the borrower; for conventional loans, the lender may give the borrower a choice between several PMI companies. PMI is added to your monthly mortgage payment; the lender transfers the PMI payment to the PMI company. PMI is required when a borrower

puts down less than 20% for a down payment. The rules about PMI also vary by loan type. For FHA loans, PMI is currently required for the life of the loan and no matter the size of your down payment. For conventional loans, the PMI policy is automatically dropped when you have 22% equity in the property per your loan amortization schedule.

Recording Fees

Fees paid to the state and/or county for recording a deed with the appropriate government agency.

Closing

Closing is also called settlement. This is the final step of buying your home and getting your mortgage. Closing includes the signing of final documents and the payments of funds, all to legally transfer the property from the seller to the buyer. Closing is generally handled by a title company or a closing attorney. Some states such as Delaware, South Carolina, Maryland, New Hampshire, Maine & Mississippi and Georgia for example require that an attorney do the closing. Usually present are the buyer, the seller, the settlement agent or closing attorney, the listing agent, and the buyer's agent.

I usually try to attend closings for all of my clients, but many lenders do not. My goal is to help facilitate a smooth, easy closing for my clients and the title company; I make myself available for questions about any of the documents. I also like to attend closings so that I can celebrate with my clients as they cross the end zone. It's a time to rejoice!

Interest

The amount you pay to the lender for borrowing money. Amortization of the interest is a portion of your monthly mortgage payment.

Late Charge

The amount of money added to your mortgage payment if it is paid late.

Lien

Any claim against a property. You cannot sell your property unless all liens are satisfied and/or released.

(13)

Loan Programs

There are a variety of loan programs to choose from. After I explain loan programs below, I'll follow up with a discussion about how and when to choose your loan program. The most common loan programs are FHA, VA, USDA, Conventional, and, Jumbo. Loan terms, which you'll learn about in detail in Chapter 15, have to do with the terms of how the loan is repaid, such as fixed-rate loans, balloon mortgages, and, ARMs. So, you might choose a conventional fixed-rate loan; "conventional" is the loan program and "fixed-rate" describes the terms of the loan.

There are different loan programs because different government entities sponsor and/or govern each of the different programs. HUD (U.S. Department of Housing and Urban Development) backs FHA loans. The Veterans Administration guarantees VA loans. Fannie Mae and Freddie Mac back most conventional loans. Note that though conventional loans are backed by Fannie Mae and Freddie Mac, they are not government loans. Thank goodness we have a variety of loan programs to choose from since one-size-fits-all has never been a good choice for anyone.

Types of Loan Programs

Government Loan Programs

VA, FHA, and USDA loans are under the group referred to as government loans. This is because they are overseen by government entities. All government loans have an upfront funding fee that is paid to the government entity that oversees that loan program.

FHA Loans

FHA – Federal Housing Administration. Governed by HUD (U.S. Department of Housing and Urban Development). An FHA loan is backed by HUD, requires mortgage insurance and has a minimum of 3.5% down payment required. It is sometimes referred to as a first time homebuyer's loan because of the ease of entry due to the low down payment. FHA loan limits vary by region across the country. FHA requires that the property be in habitable condition. To check the loan limits in your area, go to the HUD website (portal.hud.gov) and type "FHA mortgage limits" in the search bar.

Not all lenders are FHA approved. Be sure to ask your lender what loans they are approved to do.

FHA now requires monthly mortgage insurance (MI) for the life of the loan. That's whether you put down 3.5% or 20%. This is in addition to the upfront funding fee paid to HUD. Historically the FHA mortgage insurance costs change relatively often, as demonstrated by the change in January 2015 when FHA MI rates were lowered with much fanfare during an address by President Obama. Up until early 2015, the monthly mortgage insurance cost was 1.35% of the loan amount annually if you put down 3.5%. It was a little bit lower if you put down a 5% down payment, but this number has fluctuated over the past several years and may continue to fluctuate. Don't worry, the monthly mortgage insurance doesn't change after your loan is originated and closed. Future changes to monthly mortgage insurance or up-front funding fees don't affect your current loan.

The up-front funding fee can be paid in cash at closing, but most borrowers choose the option of rolling it into their loan amount. Currently the up-front funding fee for FHA loans is 1.75% of the loan amount.

FHA loans do allow for gifts for the down payment and closing costs. This means you don't have to use all of your own money to buy a house. FHA loans also allow for up to 6% help in closing costs from the seller. This, coupled with a low down payment, is why this loan is considered a first time homebuyer's loan program.

FHA loan limits vary by county across the country. To see the maximum allowable loan limit where you want to buy, go to portal.hud.gov/hudportal/HUD and type FHA mortgage limits in the search bar and fill in the relevant data.

USDA Loans

USDA loans are also called Rural Development Loans and are overseen by the U.S. Department of Agriculture. USDA loans have caps on how much household income you can make in order to qualify, as well as regional areas in which the home you are purchasing must be located. USDA loans currently have one of the lowest monthly mortgage insurance (MI) rates, but one of the highest funding fees. In addition, the funding fee is increased if you finance it by adding it to your loan. However, just like a VA loan, there is no down payment requirement for a USDA loan. That means that if you qualify, you can get into your new home with zero down payment. For more information on USDA loans, ask your lender.

You can also check out the USDA website at eligibility.sc.egov.usda.gov

Streamline Refinancing

For information about streamline refinancing a government loan, see the Refinancing section in this chapter.

VA Loans— see the chapter devoted to VA Loans and those who serve us, Chapter 14

Conventional Loans

Fannie Mae and Freddie Mac are now run by the government, but this changed in the past few years. Prior to that they were considered "quasi" government entities. They were overseen by the government, but not run by the government.

Conventional loans usually have more strict credit guidelines than government loans. They currently require at least a 5 percent down payment, unless you are a first time homebuyer, then you may be able to put down as little as 3 percent. If you put down less than 20 percent down payment, private mortgage insurance is required. However, there is no up-front funding fee. The private mortgage insurance automatically drops off once you have 22 percent equity through your amortization schedule.

Typically the conforming loan limit is $417,000, but this can vary across the country. For example, areas such as Washington, DC and Los Angeles, CA have higher loan limits for conventional loans.

Current conforming loan limits can be found on the Fannie Mae website: fanniemae.com/singlefamily/loan-limits

Jumbo Loans

Jumbo loans are conventional loans that are above the conforming loan limits. Jumbo loans have larger down payment requirements, typically 20%-30%. The credit and reserve requirements are also more strict as the loan amounts are larger than the conforming standards.

Home Equity Loan/Home Equity Line-of-Credit

Home Equity loan is a term for a variety of liens. A home equity loan can be a first lien or a second lien against your property. It gets its name because it is based on the equity in your property. For example, if your home is worth $300,000 and you have no lien on the property, you have $300,000 of equity in your home. You might want to get out $100,000 for home repairs or for your child's college tuition. You could get a Home Equity Loan based on the equity in your home. These days you must qualify with income, credit, and reserves to repay the new loan for the money you have borrowed against the equity in your home. The home equity loan went away for a few years, but it's back now; however, back with more restrictions than in past years.

Among Home Equity Loans there are a few to choose from, usually a home equity line of credit or a home equity loan. A home equity line of credit (HELOC) can be used sort of like a credit card. The interest rate is not fixed, nor is the balance. However, the credit limit is fixed, based on the equity in your home and what you qualify to pay back. You can draw money from the HELOC, pay down the principal, and, then draw out more money. Your loan terms dictate when and how much more money you may withdraw. Of course, you are required to make monthly payments based on the balance you owe, similar to a credit card.

A home equity loan is usually a fixed loan. The terms are set. There is a fixed amount you have borrowed and you must repay it over a fixed period of time. Be sure to check the terms of your loan so you understand your commitment.

Also, with Home Equity loans your taxes and property insurance are not usually escrowed. The monthly payment is interest only or principal and interest. You are expected to pay your property taxes and insurance on your own if they are not already escrowed in your primary mortgage, if you have one.

Refinancing

There are two basic types of refinance loans. One is a rate and term refinance. This means you are refinancing to get better terms on your loan. It might be a lower interest rate, a shorter loan term, or, from an adjustable rate mortgage to a fixed rate mortgage. The amount of the new refinance is equal to or less than your original loan balance. Typically, the borrower cannot receive more than $2,000 cash-back at closing.

A cash-out refinance is when you receive cash at closing or use that cash from closing to pay off other debt, such as credit card debt. You are borrowing based on the equity in your home.

Refinance loans are based on the current equity in your home. You must also meet the income, credit and asset requirements just like any other loan. The exception to this general rule is the VA IRRL. IRRL stands for Interest Rate Reduction Loan. It is not a cash-out refinance. With a VA IRRL the debt-to-income ratio is not calculated and an appraisal is not required by the VA.

Since the mortgage crash of 2007, the government has released the Home Affordable Refinance Program (HARP) that allows borrowers to refinance to a lower interest rate regardless of the equity in their home. For more details about HARP, ask your lender or check out the HARP website: makinghomeaffordable.gov/Pages/default.aspx

Streamline refinancing

Government loans have several nice options that you may be able to use to your advantage. One of those is the option for a streamline refinance. A streamline refinance lowers your interest rate. As long as current interest rates are lower than the interest rate on your loan, it may be to your advantage to consider a streamline refinance. A streamline refinance is less paperwork intensive than a purchase loan or a cash-out refinance loan. With a VA loan, your employment must be documented, but not the amount. If all closing costs can be rolled into your loan, there's no need to verify your assets— that saves you paper cuts. An appraisal is not needed either. The lender assumes that your home is worth the same or more than as the value used for your current loan. The loan amount of the new streamline loan cannot be higher than your current loan amount.

FHA also has a streamline refinance option that may not require an appraisal or credit and income qualification. Of course, be sure to consider the mortgage insurance (MI) payment on your loan versus what the new MI payment will be, as well as the remainder of the term of your loan. For example, currently FHA MI is double what it was 5 years ago, and, all new FHA loans require MI for the life of the loan instead of dropping off automatically at 78% as it did previously.

Reverse Mortgages and HECM

Reverse mortgages are only available to borrowers age 62 or over. A reverse mortgage is a mortgage loan that pays you, rather than you making monthly mortgage payments. Reverse mortgages are also known as Home Equity Conversion Mortgages (HECMs). Basically, a reverse mortgage pays you to live in your home until death. You may be able to take a lump sum, monthly payments or a combination of both. If you decide you want to move, you may pay off the reverse mortgage by paying back the money you have received from the lender.

Reverse mortgages also have different terms, depending on the lender. There are fixed rate and adjustable rate reverse mortgages. The lender should give you options once you have filled out an application. However, anyone wishing to apply for a reverse mortgage must take counseling from a government approved agency prior to applying. This requirement is to make sure that you understand how reverse mortgages work and the advantages and disadvantages of taking out a reverse mortgage.

You will be required to provide your lender with a certificate earned through a reverse mortgage (HECM) counseling program approved by the U.S. Department of Housing and Urban Development. You can find an approved counselor and information regarding reverse mortgage regulation by going to the HUD website at portal.hud.gov. Once you have navigated to this web address, type in 'reverse mortgage counseling' in the search bar on the home page.

There are two types of reverse mortgages: a reverse mortgage and reverse purchase mortgage. For the basic reverse mortgage, you must own the property, and, depending on how much you want to borrow, you must have a certain amount of equity. The total amount you can borrow is determined by your age and your equity. Credit is not a requirement to qualify for a reverse mortgage.

A reverse purchase mortgage allows you to buy a new home. For a reverse purchase mortgage, you must have a significant down payment. The amount of down payment is determined by the purchase price of the home and the amount of money you will receive from the reverse mortgage, the current interest rate and your age. Similar to a reverse mortgage, the reverse purchase mortgage then pays you to live in the home every month, until the time of death

How/When to Choose the Best Loan Program

To determine the best loan program for your situation, you need to know for what loans you are eligible. To find out which loans you are eligible for, submit your loan application and ask your licensed mortgage professional which loan programs are available for you to choose from based on your loan application. Lenders cannot determine your possible eligibility for loan programs until you have filled out a loan application, which includes reviewing your credit. It's also important to keep in mind that lenders cannot guarantee your eligibility based on your application. This is because sometimes people do not submit all information, or do not submit it correctly. Your loan application must be thoroughly reviewed during the underwriting phase of the loan process to ensure eligibility for the loan program.

Once you have submitted the application, your lender will present you with loan program options. If you qualify for more than one loan program, your licensed mortgage professional should present you with a loan program comparison worksheet. This worksheet will break down the differences in loan programs and loan terms. The loan terms will vary by loan program and have a considerable effect on the costs and monthly payments. In Chapter 15, loan terms are fully explained and you are provided with a loan comparison worksheet.

When you study your loan comparison worksheet, you'll want to make sure that you are very comfortable with your total monthly payment. When reviewing the comparison worksheet, ask your lender how certain adjustments may make beneficial changes to your costs or total monthly payment. For example, if you're eligible for a loan that does not require mortgage insurance if you have 20% equity and you were planning to put down 15%, you may want to increase your down payment to 20%.

Your decision about which loan program is best for you is affected by what kind of financial wiggle room you have at the time you wish to purchase your home. You may realize that it would be greatly advantageous to save like crazy for another 6 months to increase your down payment and lower your monthly payments and total costs. However, you may decide you don't want to risk an increase in current interest rates so you'll choose the loan program with the total monthly payment that you can comfortably pay each month and move forward with your loan application and home purchase.

You need to choose your loan program before you make an offer on the home you wish to buy. This is because your loan program is listed on the sales contract. And, you need to make sure that the property you choose is also eligible for the loan program that you want. For example, if you qualify for an FHA loan and you want to make an offer on a condominium, if the condominium is not on the FHA approved condominium list you will not be able to move forward with the sales contract because the property does not qualify for the loan. You'll either have to choose a different loan program that you qualify for or choose a different property.

Once you read the next chapter, you'll have a better understanding of how the loan program combined with the loan terms will greatly affect your choice in home loans. Your licensed mortgage professional should objectively explain all of the choices available to you and should welcome all of your questions that will help you make the absolute best choice for your situation.

Making Sense of the Jargon

ARM
Adjustable Rate Mortgage; see Chapter 15 - Loan Terms for an in-depth conversation about ARMs.

Assumable Mortgage/Assumption Clause
Assumable mortgage means that it is allowable for another person to take over your mortgage payments in exchange for ownership of the property. The person(s) taking over the payments must qualify with the lender to be eligible to assume the mortgage. Not all mortgages are assumable. VA and FHA loan programs are both assumable mortgages. Currently, conventional loans are not assumable. When another person

assumes your mortgage, they retain all of your original loan terms, such as the interest rate. This can be an attractive selling point to your buyer if interest rates were at 4% when you bought your home, but have climbed to 8% when you are ready to sell your home.

Blanket Mortgage
A blanket mortgage is a loan that is for more than one property. Blanket loans are usually commercial loans, but can be used for residential property.

Bridge Loan
A bridge loan is a short-term loan usually based on the equity in your home. People sometimes use bridge loans to get a down payment for a new home and then pay off the bridge loan once the former home is sold.

Maximum Loan Amount
The maximum loan amount is the maximum amount of money that you can borrow, based on the loan limits for a specific loan program and the maximum loan-to-value allowed for the specific loan program. Loan limits for loan programs can also be specific to the region in which you are buying the home. For example, the current loan limit (at the time of printing) for a single-family home using an FHA loan in Washington, D.C. is $625,500 while the limit for a single-family home in Duval County, FL using the same loan program is $309,350.

Mortgagee
The lender in a mortgage agreement.

Mortgagor
The borrower in a mortgage agreement

Open-End Mortgage
An open-end mortgage is like a home equity line of credit. This means that the borrower and lender have agreed that the amount of the loan can be increased if both parties come to an agreement on the amount of increase and the terms.

Predatory Lending
Predatory lending is a term describing unfair, fraudulent, or deceptive lending practices that take advantage of consumers. Predatory lenders give mortgages to people that do not have the ability to repay the loan.

Refinancing

There are two types of loan refinancing: rate and term refinance and cash-out refinance.

Rehabilitation Mortgage

A rehabilitation mortgage is a loan used to cover the cost of the home and to cover the repairs of the home. A rehabilitation mortgage requires a specific loan program, such as the FHA 203(k) or the Fannie Mae HomeStyle® renovation mortgage. If you are interested in purchasing a home that needs to be rehabilitated, such as an historic home or fixer-upper, ask your licensed loan professional what programs are currently available in the area where you wish to purchase a home.

Reverse Mortgage

A financial tool which provides seniors with funds from the equity in their homes. Generally, no payments are made on a reverse mortgage until the borrower moves or the property is sold. The final repayment obligation is designed to not exceed the proceeds from the sale of the home.

Reverse Mortgage (HECM)

Reverse mortgages are only available to borrowers age 62 or over. A reverse mortgage is a mortgage loan that pays you, rather than you making monthly mortgage payments. Reverse mortgages are also known as Home Equity Conversion Mortgages (HECMs). Basically, a reverse mortgage pays you to live in your home until death. You may be able to take a lump sum, monthly payments or a combination of both. If you decide you want to move, you may pay off the reverse mortgage by paying back the money you have received from the lender.

Secondary Financing

Secondary financing is a junior or second lien on the property. It is subordinate to the primary lien, meaning that it gets paid second if the borrower defaults. A secondary lien is typically used to avoid mortgage insurance at the time of purchasing the home. For example the buyer can avoid the mortgage insurance requirement (required if you have less than 20% equity in the home, meaning the mortgage is for more than 80% of the value of the home) by getting a primary mortgage for 80% of the purchase price/value, a secondary mortgage for 15% of the value, and paying a 5% down payment. This way, neither of the mortgages is for more than 80% of the property's value.

Second Mortgage

This is a mortgage that is secondary to the primary mortgage on the home. Secondary mortgages are also called junior mortgages. If the homeowner defaults, payment of the first mortgage takes priority over the second mortgage. The primary lender has first claim on payment from the foreclosure; if there is money left over, the secondary lender will receive full/partial payment.

Seller Financing

This means that the seller of the property loans you, the buyer, the money to buy the property. The seller "holds the note" on the home. Terms of the note and mortgage are agreed upon by the seller and the buyer. If the buyer defaults on the loan, the seller takes back the home.

Sub-Prime Loan

Typically sub-prime loans are for borrowers with a credit score below 620. Sub-prime loans have higher interest rates than the prevailing market rate because these borrowers are considered a higher risk to the lender. The phrase sub-prime lending is also used to describe loan programs or lenders that use less rigorous underwriting requirements so that they give loans to people that do not qualify for most loan programs.

(14)

VA Loans

First of all, to all of you who have served or are currently serving in the Military; thank you for your service. I cannot say this too many times or with enough sincere enthusiasm. If it weren't for your dedicated service to our country, I know I would not have the amazing life that I am so fortunate to enjoy here in the U.S. Thank you!

Your unwavering service to our country gives you quite a few benefits. One of these benefits is the VA Loan. In my humble opinion, it is by far the best loan available and you have earned it. It is one of the few loans that does not require a down payment. So, you are able to finance 100% of your purchase. There is an upfront funding fee for VA loans. The funding fee can be waived if you are disabled in the line of duty. If you choose to have a down payment, the funding fee decreases on a sliding scale based on the amount of money you put down.

Type of Veteran	Down Payment	% for First Time Use	% for Subsequent Use
Regular Military	None	2.15%	3.3%"
	5% or more	1.5%	1.5%
	10% or more	1.25%	1.25%
Reserves/ Natinal Guard	None	2.4%	3.3%*
	5% or more	1.75%	1.75%
	10% or more	1.5%	1.5%

Source: U.S. VA
benefits.va.gov/homeloans/documents/docs/funding_fee_table.pdf

For the all the funding fees (purchase, construction, cash-out refinances and Interest Rate Reduction Loans) check with the U.S. Department of Veterans Affairs. Go to the VA website at benefits.va.gov and type "loan fees home loans" in the search bar.

VA Loan with Funding Fee ($0 Down Payment)

Purchase Price $300,000.00
Down Payment.. $0.00
Base Loan Amount $300,000.00
Funding Fee of 2.15%... $6,450.00

Total Loan Amount = ... $306,450.00

Most loans require you to pay a monthly mortgage insurance premium if you put down less than a twenty percent down payment. With the VA Loan, you are not required to pay this monthly mortgage insurance fee; the VA insures the loan for you at no monthly cost to you.

In addition, the limits on the amount of seller help allowed are the most lenient of all loan types. Per the VA, the seller's concessions (seller help) cannot exceed 4% of the loan. However, only some types of costs fall under this rule. Examples of costs that fall under the 4% cap are pre-paid closing costs, the VA funding fee, payoff of credit balances or judgments for the Veteran getting the loan, and, funds for temporary "buy downs." A fee that the seller can pay for that is not subject to the 4% cap is discount points.

The VA protects you from miscellaneous junk fees, such as the WDO/Pest Inspection fee, notary fee, and, commitment fee. Below are a few lists that provide examples of what the VA buyer is allowed and not allowed to pay for when getting a VA loan. These lists, gleaned from the Veterans Benefits Administration website at vba.va.gov, are illustrative lists only and should not be taken as comprehensive. Michael J. Frueh, Director of Loan Guaranty Service, Veterans Benefits Administration, U.S. Department of Veterans Affairs, directs anyone that may be eligible for a VA Loan to visit the official VA Home Loans website at benefits.va.gov/homeloans, and, to work with a knowledgeable lender that can provide a comprehensive and up-to-date list of all allowable and non-allowable fees for VA loans.

Allowable Fees

The following fees are always allowed regardless of the 1% origination fee being charged:

- Appraisal fee – per allowable maximum appraisal fee schedule for state

- Compliance inspection – only if required by the NOV (notice of value)

- Credit report – in most cases it should not exceed $50

- Recording fees, taxes and stamps

- Prorated tax and insurance escrow

- Hazard insurance – if it was not paid directly out of pocket by veteran outside closing

- Survey and plot plan

- Title insurance, title policy, title exam, title search, title endorsement and any fees required to prepare title work

- Environmental Protection lien endorsement

- 1% origination fee

- VA funding fee

- Discount points

- Closing protection letter – sometimes just listed as "CPL" (should not exceed $35, except in Pennsylvania it is $75)

- Interthinx DISSCO fraud protection report

- MERS fee

- Well and Septic inspection fees

- Express mail fees (only for cash-out refinances and IRRRL's) – actual cost should be reasonable. If not question it (over $50 should be questioned – ask for actual invoice)

Sometimes we're not the only ones in search of a home, even our furry friends need help.
For more information visit nopawsleftbehind.org

Un-Allowable Fees

The following fees are always un-allowed if the
1% origination fee is charged:

- Lender's appraisal – the veteran can only be charged for 1 appraisal unless VA deemed a second appraisal mandatory

- Lender's inspection – if it is not required on the appraisal/NOV, it can not be charged to the veteran

- Settlement fee, escrow fee, closing fee

- Document preparation fee

- Underwriting fee

- Processing fee

- Application fee – a veteran can be charged up front the cost of the appraisal and credit report to ensure the loan officer is not stuck with those fees if the veteran walks away from the deal.

- Pest inspection fee

- Attorney fees if for something other than title work

- Assignment fee

- Copying fee

- E-mail fee

- Fax fee

- Photographs

- Postage fees if not a cash-out refinance or IRRRL

- Amortization schedule

- Notary fee

- Commitment fee

- Trustee fee

- Truth in lending fee

- Mortgage broker fee

- Tax service fee

The above list is not all inclusive. You may find something other than those listed. These fees cannot be charged by the lender, title company or investor. Please refer those to the Loan Officer for review.

Unless a fee is mandated by a city, county or state, and it is not on the allowable fee list, it cannot be charged to the veteran if a 1% origination fee was charged.

If the 1% origination fee was not charged, the above list of unallowable fees can be charged to the veteran provided they do not exceed 1%. If the lender chose to charge the veteran a ½% origination fee, then items from the unallowable list can be charged provided they do not exceed 0.5% of the loan amount.

Never-Allowable Fees

Finally, there are some fees that can never be paid by the veteran regardless of whether the 1% origination fee was paid or not. Those are:

- Termite/pest inspection
- Attorney fee charged as a benefit to the lender
- Mortgage broker fee
- Real estate agent commission
- Prepayment penalties
- HUD/FHA inspection fees for builders

Not all lenders are familiar with the intricacies of VA Loans; there are specialists that can help you. You should always try to work with a certified Military Relocation Professional (a designation earned through certification by the National Association of REALTORS®) if you are applying for a VA loan. This applies to real estate agents and lenders. Those with the Military Relocation Professional certification are skilled in working with VA buyers, have taken specific education in order to serve you, and, have passed additional tests in order to be awarded the MRP certification. These professionals will know and understand terms like BAH (Base Allowance for Housing), PCS (Permanent Change of Station), Conus (Continental US), OConus (Outside Continental US) and COLA (Cost-of-Living Adjustment).

There are additional benefits of VA Loans, such as multiple use, refinance, loan assumption, splitting entitlement between multiple properties, and, being able to go over the VA Loan Limits. Let's talk more about these VA Loan Options.

Multiple Use

As long as your entitlement is restored each time you use a VA loan, you can use your VA privileges again and again. The funding fee is increased after the first use (remember, if you receive disability from the VA, the funding fee may be waived).

Assumption

Your VA loan is assumable. That means that if you choose to sell your home, the buyer may qualify to assume your loan. The buyer will have to qualify for the loan, but they are able to assume the loan with your loan terms. Why would this be attractive to your buyer? Well, let's say that when you bought your home you qualified for an interest rate of 3.875%. When you list your home for sale, perhaps interest rates have jumped to 8.0%. Your buyer will save lots of money if they assume your low 3.875% payment! Be careful! If your buyer assumes your VA loan, your VA loan benefit is still tied to that home and may hinder your eligibility for future use of your VA loan benefits. Be sure to research the pros and cons of letting anyone assume your VA loan. FHA loans are also assumable.

However, there is one way to transfer the liability from the veteran selling the home to the veteran buying the home when the loan is assumed; that is when a qualified veteran assumes the loan and the VA does a Release of Liability, the veteran buying the home takes over all aspects of the prior loan.

Splitting Entitlement

Splitting Entitlement between multiple properties — if you used your VA benefits to purchase a home in Virginia Beach, VA and you get transferred to Jacksonville, FL, you may be eligible to use your VA benefits again to purchase a home in Jacksonville. This will depend on the VA loan limits in the area, your remaining VA entitlement, and, the additional loan amount you are seeking. Ask me or ask your lender for details. Just like conventional loans and FHA loans, VA Loan Limits vary by regions in the country.

You can find the current list of VA Guaranty loan limits online by entering "county loan limits" in the search bar at benefits.va.gov.

As long as you have enough entitlement and equity, you can go over the VA Guaranteed Loan limits. For example, if the loan limit in

Washington, DC is $625,500.00, the maximum base loan amount is $625,500.00. If your sales price is $800,000.00 and you put down a 25% down payment (and you have enough eligibility), you may qualify for a VA loan amount of $772,637.00.

Example: VA Loan Over Guaranteed Limit
(VA Loan Over the Loan Limits in Washington, D.C.)

Sales Price..$800,000.00
D.C. Loan Limit..$625,500.00
Difference...$174,500.00

$174,500.00 x 0.25 = $43,625.00, minimum down payment

Sales Price..$800,000.00
25% of Difference = Down Payment............................($43,625.00)
Base Loan Amount..$756,375.00
Base Loan Amount..$756,375.00
Plus Funding fee of 2.15%..$16,262.00

Total Loan Amount = ...$772,637.00

Interview with Veterans Benefits Administration

Michael J. Frueh is the Director of Loan Guaranty Service, Veterans Benefits Administration, U.S. Department of Veterans Affairs. Mark Connors is Lender Liaison for loan policy and valuation loan guaranty services at the Loan Guaranty Service of the Veterans Benefits Administration at the U.S. Department of Veterans Affairs.

This is an excerpt of an extensive and informative interview that the author conducted with Mr. Frueh and Mr. Connors. To watch the full interview or read the transcript, go to bestmortgagebook.com/veterans. There's a wealth of information in the extended interview and anyone that may be eligible for a VA loan is encouraged to make use of this resource. Did you serve in the U.S. military? Did your spouse serve in the U.S. military? Please, watch this video!

Elysia: Hi, I'm Elysia Stobbe and I'm here at the Department of Veterans Affairs today interviewing two of their top brass with some great questions for VA home-buyers. If you could introduce yourselves please.

Michael J. Frueh: Hi, I'm Mike Frueh. I'm the Director of the VA Loan Program here in D.C.

Mark Connors: Hi, I'm Mark Connors. I'm the Lender Liaison in D.C.

Elysia: Great! So, we put together a few questions we thought would be helpful for either first time users of their VA Home Loan benefits or anybody who's actually used it before and maybe had questions and had any kind of challenges. The idea is to make it smoother for the veteran as they purchase a home. So, the first question I have is for Mark. What is something that lenders forget to tell people that are looking for VA loans or interested in using their VA loan benefits?

Mark Connors: Well, actually I don't know that I would say what they forget to tell the veteran, but rather what they forget to ask the veteran and just a simple, have you served? Or are you a veteran? Or do you know if you qualify for the VA home loan program? That is something that we would encourage everybody in the industry to ask the veterans, have you served? Do you know if you may be eligible for the home loan benefit? Because it doesn't do the veteran any good to find out after they have purchased a home that they qualified for the home loan benefit.

Elysia: So, you think there's probably a portion out there that just by the loan origination process, and, when they're doing the application, that the lenders aren't asking those questions?

Mark Connors: Absolutely, yes, and again we encourage lenders or Realtors® that that's the question that we would like to get across more than anything.

Michael J. Frueh: I agree and there are even veterans out there that have used the benefit in the past that have bought a home before that don't know that they can use it again. So it's not just a single-use program. There are probably a lot of real estate agents out there, and lenders, that don't know it's available multiple times throughout a veteran's life. That's something that we've been trying to overcome with education. Letting people know that this is a comprehensive benefit that can help veterans at any stage in their life. It's not a first time home buying program; it's an anytime you want to buy a home buying program.

Elysia: Do either of you have any inspirational stories about the VA and what it's done to help Veterans?

Michael J. Frueh: I have one that I always think about. The home loan benefit is actually three benefits. One, it helps veterans purchase a home: purchase a home that's geared for their success, so that they're not stretching too much to buy a home they can't afford, they're not putting too much money down in down payment so they have money in reserves. Two, we have a group of people that help veterans keep their homes if they have problems. Three, we help severely wounded veterans adapt their homes, so they can actually live independently in the home where they want to live, so they're not forced to live in home hospital care or nursing care.

The second benefit, retaining a home-- we have 150 people around the country that are there to help veterans when things happen. One veteran in particular in Arizona got cancer and he couldn't go to work, so he couldn't make his mortgage payment. He had a family. He talked to us, we said we know what's going on, we'll talk to your mortgage bank, don't worry about your home, worry about getting well. So, we talked to his bank, the bank said, don't worry while he's going through treatment, we'll defer his payments and we'll work with him later to try to get caught up. He wrote a letter that I still have today, that said of all the stuff he was worried about, his cancer was the least of his worries. His biggest worry was that his wife and his children wouldn't have a home to live in because he was going through this treatment. He said the amount of worry we took out of his life probably helped him overcome the cancer. He was a success story, got better, went back to work, reinstated his loan, and lived in his home. He said that the big worry we took out of his life totally transformed his attitude at the time.

Elysia: That's a great story.

Michael J. Frueh: It made me feel good.

Mark Connors: Mr. Frueh talked about three parts and the way he likes to say it is easy to remember, so our mission is to help veterans obtain, retain and adapt. Perhaps another inspirational story is the 20th million loan.

Michael J. Frueh: We just hit our 21st million loan yesterday. Two years ago this October we hit our 20th million loan. Our 20th million loan didn't go to a veteran or a service member; it went to a surviving spouse. The surviving spouse is a woman named Beth Carpenter who lives in Springfield, Virginia with her little boy. Her husband passed away while he was in service. So, she's going through all the grief that people go through for losing a spouse and her son had just lost his father. Someone had told her here's a benefit you have as a surviving spouse. You can still use your husband's VA home loan benefit to buy a home without a down payment.

By telling her that, it was her Realtor® I think that let her know, she actually looked for a home and found a home that she couldn't have bought otherwise that she was able to buy without a down payment. Our Under Secretary, myself, and several other people went out to her house to celebrate when she had moved in to say we're very happy we're able to help her and her family get a house. But she was the 20th million, so there were 20 million others before her, including surviving spouses; and, again she wouldn't have known about it if someone didn't bring it up, and say "Oh your husband served, maybe you qualify for this benefit." It's even more reason to get the word out to ask that question.

Elysia: It's just like you were saying earlier, so not only "have you served" but, "have you or your spouse served?"

To watch the full interview go to bestmortgagebook.com/veterans.

For more VA Loan Guarantee information see the following websites:

benefits.va.gov/homeloans

ebenefits.va.gov

ebenefits.va.gov/ebenefits/about

To support the USO, go here to donate:
https://secure.uso.org/?sc=WEBDONATION&ta=6005

(15)

Loan Terms

Loan terms affect the overall cost of your loan, so all of the terms, not just the percentage rate, are important to calculate and compare. At the end of this chapter, you'll find a worksheet that will help you compare the overall cost of loans that you are considering. Loan terms state the parameters of loan repayment; these parameters affect the overall price of your loan. Parameters of repayment include the length of the loan (also called the life); interest rate; and, loan term features such as ARMs or balloons. Note that two meanings of the word 'term' are used in speaking about mortgages: (1) 'term' meaning the length of time, and, (2) 'terms' meaning the scope and parameters of your loan agreement.

Loan terms can be dictated by the loan program and by the lender. What does that mean? Well, not all lenders offer all the terms available for each loan type. Some lenders only offer fixed terms, such as 15- and 30-year terms. Some also offer ARMs and balloons. It's important to ask questions about loan terms when you are applying for your loan so you know what options you have to choose from.

Loan terms are important to consider depending on what's going on in your life and what you expect in the upcoming years. Let's say that you have a job that requires you to move every 4 years. Then you may want to consider a 3- or 5-year ARM. That means that your interest rate will be fixed for the first 3 or 5 years of your mortgage. If you plan on selling and moving in less than 3-5 years, it's worth considering an ARM since the initial interest rate is usually lower than a fixed interest rate. If you don't move around much, a fixed interest rate may be a good option for you. A fixed interest rate does not change during the life of the loan.

Below you'll find a breakdown of loan terms (length and interest rate) and an explanation of the most common loan term features (ARMs, balloons, fixed, and, interest only). After that there's a Q&A section, followed by the Understanding the Lingo section, and then your Loan Comparison Worksheet.

Key Loan Terms

Length of the Loan
(30, 15, 10 years, etc.). This is how long the loan is amortized, or how many years it will take you to repay the principal and interest of the loan. This is also called the life of the loan. The shorter the term, the less time you have to pay back the loan, so the higher your monthly payment. Most people qualify for the most house with a 30-year fixed mortgage since they have the longest time period to pay back the loan. If you are closer to retirement, you may qualify for and choose a shorter term such as a 15-year fixed term; this will allow you to pay off your home about the same time as you retire, therefore reducing your household expenses as you hypothetically have less income. The bottom line is that you choose a payment that you can afford and that doesn't stress you out each month. Remember to take into consideration the full PITI (discussed in detail in chapter 7).

Interest Rate
That's important to know! At what interest rate will your monthly payments be calculated? The interest rate is a percentage rate that you pay to the lender for use of their money to buy the home. It's the cost of borrowing the money. Interest rates can vary by lender. Interest rates are calculated on loan-to-value, credit score, loan term, loan program, loan size, and, state — to name a few variables. Ask your lender if it is possible to get a lower rate and have them explain why or why not.

For example, I was speaking with my friend Mary last week; she called to say that she was quoted 4.125% by another lender and thought the interest rate was not very competitive. For the loan type and loan amount, it was competitive. When I asked why Mary thought it was not a competitive rate, her answer was that she spoke with her friend Bob the week before who said he just closed on a home and their rate was 3.875%. At first glance, you can easily see why my friend Mary thought the 4.125% was not competitive. Well, the 3.875% was a government rate (which are currently lower than conventional interest rates) and hers was a conventional loan. Also, the 3.875% may have been a shorter loan term, as well. In addition, her friend Bob may have locked his loan 30 days prior when interest rates were lower.

ARM Mortgages

ARM stands for adjustable rate mortgage. It's just what it sounds like — adjustable — your interest rate adjusts periodically during the course of the loan. But, the term is fixed, usually a 30-year repayment period. During the life of the loan the interest rate will change based on the index rate. These are also referred to as adjustable mortgage loans (AMLs) or variable-rate mortgages (VRMs). These mortgage loans usually have changing interest rates after a set period of time; the change in interest rate happens at a predetermined time and then adjusts periodically, again at predetermined times.

Why would you choose an ARM? ARMs' introductory fixed period have a lower interest rate than a fixed rate. In exchange for the lower interest rate, you have volatility. An ARM may be worth considering if you know that you will pay off or sell your home in less than five years before your ARM interest rate adjusts or adjusts too much. Let's say that you know you have a job that requires you to move every 4 years. Then you may want to consider a 3- or 5-year ARM. That means that your interest rate will be fixed for the first 3 or 5 years of your mortgage.

If you plan on selling and moving before the adjustment date, it's worth considering an ARM, since the initial interest rate is usually lower than a fixed interest rate. If you don't move around much, then a fixed interest rate may be a good option for you. A fixed interest rate does not change during the life of the loan. Adjustable rate mortgages are more for risk takers. If you are more conservative, then a fixed rate may be right for you.

ARMs are priced based on an index and a margin. The margin is the profit for the lender. These terms are clearly spelled out in your note. The index can be based on the LIBOR, COFI, or the Prime Rate, and, the margin is risk-based profit pricing that the lender determines based on your credit score and other parameters. The index plus the margin is your variable interest rate. For example, if the prime rate is 0.75% and the margin is 3.0%, your introductory interest rate will be 3.75%. If you want to get an idea of what may happen and the level of volatility of an index, you can research the past performance of the specific index.

If you have an index of 3.25% and a margin of 0.75%, then your rate will be 4.0%. This is usually amortized over a 30-year period. So, if you have a principal loan amount of $300,000 and your rate is 4.0%, then your Principal & Interest payment would be $1,432.25. Some ARMs have a teaser rate. When the rate changes, ARM monthly payments increase or decrease at intervals determined by the lender; the change in monthly payment amount, however, is usually subject to a cap.

There are usually caps for each adjustment period, as well as an overall cap. For example, you could have a 2/5 cap. That means that the maximum percentage that the interest rate can adjust is 2% at each pre-determined interval and 5% overall. Keep in mind that these adjustments can be UP or DOWN. If the index tied to your note is now less than the index was during the prior period, then your interest rate will go down. If the index tied to your note is now higher, then your interest rate will go up. Make sense? If not, just email our team at info@bestmortgagebook.com.

Another part of an ARM mortgage is the duration of the fixed interest rate before the lender can change the rate, and also by how much the rate can be adjusted. The duration of the fixed interest rate is decided by the ARM you choose. The shorter the initial period before adjustment, the lower the interest rate. A 3/1 ARM has an interest rate that is fixed for the first 3 years of the loan; the interest rate will then adjust every year following the completion of the initial three years. ARMs can also adjust on a 6-month basis. How much the rate adjusts is always tied to the index associated with your note and the margin. (How does a rate get associated with your loan? The interest rate is the index plus the margin.)

If your index is based on the prime rate and it has increased to 2.0% when it's time for your loan to adjust and your margin is 3.0%, then your new interest rate will be 5.0%. If the prime rate has declined and is 0.25% and your margin is 3.0%, then your new interest rate will be 3.25% for that next period. ARMs also have CAPS to protect you from payment shock. Usually the maximum an ARM can adjust is 2%-5% in any given direction. ARMs also have a floor that protects the lender from losing too much money. The floor is the bottom of where the interest rate can adjust. ARMs usually have prepayment penalties associated with them. Prepayment penalties may be included in your loan terms and are discussed in further detail in the next chapter.

Balloon Mortgages

A balloon mortgage means that the interest rate and terms are fixed until a certain time (typically 7 years) and then payment is due in full. A balloon mortgage might be worth considering if you know you will try to sell your home before the balloon matures or you plan to pay it off in full. A balloon mortgage, similar to an ARM, may have a lower interest rate than a fixed term loan. The lower interest rate is fixed for the portion of the loan before the balloon is due.

This will result in a lower monthly payment and may be attractive to you as a borrower. Keep in mind that when the balloon is due, you must pay it in full. The balloon mortgage can be amortized over 30 or 15 years, then it balloons and you must pay the remaining balance, or, you can refinance if you are eligible. For example, your loan could be amortized over 30 years, but due in 15 years. That's an example of a balloon. Lot loans can often have that type of balloon. A lot loan is a loan that uses raw land as collateral.

This strategy may work for you if you plan to own your home for a shorter time period, or, if you have a higher risk tolerance. If you are still in your home when the balloon is due and you are not able to pay it in full or sell your home to pay it in full, you may be able to refinance the loan into another balloon or into a fixed term loan.

Fixed Rate Mortgages

A fixed-rate mortgage means that the terms of the loan, such as interest rate and term, are fixed. A 30-year fixed and 15-year fixed are the most common fixed-rate mortgages, but there are also 20-, 25-, and 10-year fixed mortgages. Keep in mind that although your loan principal and interest may be fixed, there are parts of your monthly payment that will always be subject to change.

What? Yes, it's true. Even if you have a fixed rate, your escrows will change. Your property taxes may change annually. Expect larger increases if you have not homesteaded your property. (See Homesteading under the Property Tax Changes paragraph at the end of Chapter 3 for more Information about Homesteading.) Your homeowners insurance may change annually. Your homeowners association dues and condo fees (if you live in a PUD or a condo) may change annually. If you have mortgage insurance, it may be removed (depending on your loan type) when you have a certain amount of equity in your home. Be sure to ask your licensed trusted mortgage banker for more details.

Interest-Only Loans and Home Equity Loans

There are also interest only loans. Most home equity lines of credit are interest-only loans and have variable interest rates. A home equity loan can be in first position, but is usually in 2nd position behind your primary mortgage. A home equity loan can be a fixed loan (fixed repayment time and terms) or a line of credit. With an interest-only home equity line of credit, you are responsible to repay the principal and interest, but you are only required to pay the interest each month for a certain period of time.

This means that either your payment will balloon or your entire loan may balloon. In addition, a home equity line of credit works a bit like a credit card. You can draw money from it, pay down the principal, and, then draw out more money. Your loan terms dictate when and how much more money you may withdraw. Of course, you are required to make monthly payments based on the balance you owe, similar to a credit card.

Q&A Session

Q: Why should borrowers be informed about loan terms before starting the whole process? How can they use this knowledge to their advantage?

Elysia: Understanding loan terms helps you determine your payment and how long you will pay the loan, and, you'll know if your principal and interest will be fixed or change while you are repaying the loan. Since a 15-year loan term is shorter than a 30-year loan term, the payment is higher but the interest rate is probably lower (because the term is shorter). This is important to consider since this is an obligation for a long time.

Terms are also important to consider depending where you are in your career. Lets say you are closer to retirement. You may consider a 15-year loan term, to pay off before you retire, so that you don't have a mortgage payment when you may not be in your peak earning years. Or, you may want a 30-year fixed so you can save more for your retirement. Everyone's situation is different. Only you can decide what's right for you.

Q: What should loan applicants keep an eye out for, in relation to loan terms, throughout the process?

Elysia: Certain disclosures are required for ARMs and all the terms of the loan will be in your NOTE as well as the TIL (Truth in Lending).

Q: What questions should applicants ask the lender?

Elysia: What's my TOTAL monthly payment? What does that include? What parts of my monthly payment may change over time? Lenders should review all parts of the monthly payment with you to let you know what may change, why, and, when.

Q: How does monthly payment affect getting to closing?

Elysia: The monthly payment of the loan affects your debt-to-income ratio. If your interest rate is floating and the rate goes up, your debt-to-income ratio may become too high and then you may no longer qualify for the loan.

Q: When should applicants lock the rate?

Elysia: When you should lock and how long you should lock depends on a few factors. For example, what is the closing date in your sales contract? If you are planning to close in 45 days and lock the 2nd day into your sales contract, you need to lock for 45 days, not 15 or 30 days, if you want the current interest rate. Otherwise, that locked interest rate will expire and you will be paying to extend it or you'll have to let the rate float with the market.

I'm very conservative, so for my personal loans, if I'm happy with the total payment and the interest rate, I lock it through the closing day of my sales contract. However, if you are a risk-taker and want to gamble that interest rates may go down and you will be happier with a lower payment, you can float your loan. Keep in mind that if your interest rate is not locked and it is floating, then your interest rate can go up as well as down.

Q: How do loan terms affect the life of my loan?

Elysia: Loan terms determine how much you will pay each month, if that will change, when, how often, and, how much.

Q: Can loan terms change? If so, when/why?

Elysia: Yes, loan terms can change depending on the length of the loan, if it is an ARM or if it is a balloon. When comparing the loan program choices given to you by your lender, ask which programs include terms that may change.

Making Sense of the Jargon

Acceleration

This is the right of the lender to demand full payment on the balance of your mortgage loan. The terms of acceleration are in your note. An example of why a lender could demand payment is default (not paying) on your mortgage. The lender may also have the right to demand payment if the way the title was recorded has changed. For example, if you closed on your loan in your name, but after the closing you quit claimed it into an LLC or someone else's name, the lender may invoke the acceleration clause.

Additional Principal Payment

This is any additional money that you pay on a monthly mortgage payment that is over and above the set amount due for the monthly payment. This extra money that you may choose to pay is applied to your loan principal. So, if you pay extra sometimes, you can shorten the length of time it takes to repay your loan. Please note, even if you pay over the amount required each month, you may NOT skip a mortgage payment; any extra payments do not count as a reserve towards a rainy day.

You will be penalized if you do not make your monthly payment, even if you have made higher than required payments in the past. If your principal and interest payment is $1,500 per month and you pay $1,700, you should note in your payment that the additional $200 should be applied to the principal balance. Some people choose to make additional principal payments to work towards paying off the loan sooner than the original time period chosen in the loan terms.

Adjustment Date

The adjustment date is the actual date that the interest rate is changed for an ARM. This date is predetermined by the terms of your note. For example, if you close on your mortgage on January 15th, 2015, and your ARM is due for its first adjustment in five years, then on January 15, 2020 you will have a new interest rate. January 15, 2020 is your adjustment date.

Adjustment Index

The published market index used to calculate the interest rate of an ARM at the time of origination or adjustment. The index can be COFI, Prime Rate, Libor or another chosen by your lender. The index and margin determine your interest rate.

INDEX + MARGIN = INTEREST RATE

Adjustment Interval

This is the amount of time between the interest rate change and the monthly payment for an ARM. The interval is usually every one, three, or, five years depending on the index. For example, if your adjustment interval is 5/1, then your initial interest rate is fixed for the first five years of the loan and then will adjust every year thereafter. If it is a 5/6, then your initial interest rate is fixed for the first five years of the loan and then will adjust every six months thereafter. Thought I was going to say 6 years, right? Not in this case. What? Not all mortgage terms and lingo make sense, so be sure to ASK your lender what the terms actually mean.

Amortization

Amortization is a mathematical rendering of a schedule for loan repayment. There are different ways of calculating amortization payments; usually the principal and interest are amortized together into monthly payments, but with interest-only loans, only the interest is amortized and paid monthly. Your monthly mortgage payment is derived from the amortization of the loan amount plus interest.

Annual Percentage Rate (APR)

Annual percentage rate is the cost of credit put in an annualized percentage form. APR is the cost of having a mortgage versus if you simply paid cash for the home. The APR on your loan includes fees from the lender and the title company that are required to close your loan. The APR is not your note rate. APR is sometimes used for comparison-shopping among lenders. It's important to keep in mind that government loans will have higher APRs because they include funding fees to close your loan. In addition, if you have mortgage insurance it will also increase your APR.

Bridge Loan (or Swing Loan)

A bridge or swing loan is a short-term loan that is paid off quickly; these are usually used while waiting for a long-term loan to be processed. You may consider a bridge loan if you are purchasing property, but have not sold your current property. These are rarely available these days and are a bit risky since you are obtaining a new loan while still obligated to your current mortgage. Not for the faint of heart.

Caps (Interest)

This is the percentage that your interest rate can adjust in an ARM (Adjustable Rate Mortgage). It's a consumer safeguard on an ARM that limits the amount the interest rate may change per year. There are usually caps for each adjustment period, as well as an overall or lifetime cap. For example, you could have a 2/5 cap. That means that the maximum percentage that the interest rate can adjust is 2% at each interval and 5% over the life of the loan. Keep in mind that these adjustments can be UP or DOWN. If the index tied to your note is less than the index was prior, then your interest rate will go down. If the index tied to your note is higher, then your interest rate will go up.

Cap (Payment)

A payment cap is a limit placed on the amount that your monthly payment can increase or decrease.

Conversion Clause

A conversion clause is an option that may be included in ARM that will allow you to convert the ARM to a fixed-rate mortgage later in the life of your loan.

Convertible ARM

A convertible ARM is an ARM that includes a conversion clause.

Cost of Funds Index (COFI)

The 11th District Cost of Funds Index was first introduced in December of 1982. It is a National Monthly Median Cost of Funds defined as interest (dividends) paid or accrued on deposits for Western American Financial Institutions. It is calculated on the last day of the month.

Fixed Rate Mortgage

A mortgage with payments that remain the same throughout the life of the loan because the interest rate and other terms are fixed and do not change. Keep in mind that this refers to the principal and interest payments. This does not include your escrows for property taxes, homeowners insurance, condo fees, or, HOA fees. Those are NOT fixed for the life of the loan. Don't make the mistake of confusing the two. Ask your lender what parts of your mortgage payment may change, how much, when, and, why. If you have a fixed rate mortgage, the 5th box on the GFE entitled "Summary of your loan" will be checked "NO".

Good Faith Estimate (GFE)

A Good Faith Estimate is a summary of your loan costs. It is only an estimate, not your final costs of closing. There are quite a few things that can change along the way to closing. The 2010 GFE which is currently required to be used by lenders and brokers has 3 groups of fees. Box A is the lender or broker's charges. Box B is all other charges. Box C is the total of Box A and B.

In August of 2015, new documents will replace the GFE and HUD-1. The GFE will be replaced by the New Loan Estimate. The HUD-1 will be replaced by the New Closing Disclosure.

Currently the 2010 GFE is being used. Here is a link to see what it looks like: hud.gov/offices/hsg/ramh/res/gfeform.pdf

Look for the sample GFE and the checklist for understanding the GFE at the end of this chapter.

Graduated Payment Mortgages

Graduated payment is a term on your mortgage note that provides for increasing the monthly payment over time until reaching a fixed payment amount. Graduated payments is an option to pay off the loan sooner than you would if you had kept the lower payment amount. If you expect to increase your income over time, a graduated payment mortgage may be a good term option.

Federal Funds Rate

The overnight interest rate at which banks (depository institutions) in the U.S. lend each other money. The rate is determined by the Federal Reserve. Remember that The Fed is not associated with the government, it's the King of the Banks. The actual interest rate that banks lend to each other may change slightly from The Fed's target, but it's usually very close. The FOMC (Federal Open Market Committee) determines when and how much the rate needs to be adjusted. Also called the Federal Funds Target Rate or Intended Federal Funds Rate or Market Federal Funds Rate. That's a lot of AKA's!

Float
The act of allowing an interest rate and discount points to fluctuate with changes in the market. When your loan is originated you can choose to lock or float your interest rate. If you float, your interest rate is at the mercy of the market. If you choose to lock it, it is locked for a period of time, usually 30, 45 or 60 days. You must close on your loan within that time frame or you may be charged a fee for a lock extension. This is important stuff! Ask your lender if your interest rate is floating or locked. They MUST send you loan disclosures that show if your interest rate is floating or locked. This is legally required.

Interest
A fee charged for the use of borrowing money. This is what you pay the lender for the privilege of using their money instead of your own.

Interest Rate
The amount of interest charged on a monthly loan payment, expressed as a percentage.

Late Payment Charges
The penalty the homeowner must pay when a mortgage payment is made after the due date grace period. This is usually 5% for a conventional loan and 4% for a government loan. Some states may have additional restrictions on the percentage that the bank can charge you for paying late. Most late penalties apply on the 15th of the month if your mortgage is due on the 1st.

Life Cap
A limit on the range interest rates can increase or decrease over the life of an adjustable-rate mortgage (ARM). For example, you could have a 2/5 cap. That means that the maximum percentage that the interest rate can adjust is 5% over the life of the loan and 2% at each interval. Keep in mind that these adjustments can be UP or DOWN. If the index tied to your note is less than the index was, then your interest rate will go down. If the index tied to your note is higher, then your interest rate will go up.

Lifetime Payment Cap

The lifetime payment cap is the maximum amount, in percentage terms, which an adjustable rate mortgage can increase.

Lifetime Rate Cap

The highest or lowest a rate an Adjustable Rate Mortgage can reach for the life of the loan.

Loan

Money borrowed that is usually repaid with interest. In the case of a mortgage, it is secured by real property.

Loan Acceleration

An acceleration clause in a loan document is a statement in a mortgage that gives the lender the right to demand payment of the entire outstanding balance if a monthly payment is missed. There may be other circumstances that cause a loan to accelerate such as a change in title.

Lock-In

See Rate Lock below.

LIBOR Index

The LIBOR (London Interbank Offered Rate) Index is based on the daily average of interbank offered rates in London. What does that mean? It's the percentage at which banks in London loan each other money on the wholesale market. There are a variety of LIBOR rate averages, such as 1-month, 3-month, 6-month, and, 1-year. Even though it's based in Europe, it is used in U.S. Capital markets and is one of the standards used in order to set interest rates such as ARMs.

Margin

The number of percentage points the lender adds to the index rate to calculate the ARM interest rate at each adjustment. This is the profit for the lender.

Maturity

Maturity is the scheduled end-date of your loan, the date the loan is scheduled to be paid in full.

Mortgage-Backed Security (MBS)

A mortgage-backed security is an investment product that is made up of a group of mortgages.

Mortgage Interest Deduction

The interest cost of a mortgage, which is a tax deductible expense in most cases. The interest reduces the taxable income of taxpayers. Consult with a tax specialist, preferably a CPA (Certified Public Accountant), to see how this may benefit you.

Mortgage Modification

An option that the borrower may be able to take advantage of to extend the term of the loan and/or reduce the interest rate, which in turn reduces the monthly payment. These were popular after the mortgage meltdown of 2007. They were so popular that sub industries in the mortgage arena were created to facilitate the execution of these mortgage modifications. However, a mortgage may also be modified for other reasons besides loss mitigation.

Mortgage Note

A legal document obligating a borrower to repay a loan at a stated interest rate during a specified period; the agreement is secured by a mortgage that is recorded in the public records along with the deed. This has all the details of how, when & what you will be repaying your mortgage.

Mortgagee

The lender in a mortgage agreement. Usually a mortgage lender, bank, credit union, sometimes the seller of the property.

Mortgagor

The borrower in a mortgage agreement. This means YOU!

Negative Amortization

Amortization means that monthly payments are large enough to pay the interest and reduce the principal on your mortgage. Negative amortization occurs when the monthly payments do not cover all of the interest cost. The interest cost that isn't covered is added to the unpaid principal balance. This means that even after making many payments, you could owe more than you did at the beginning of the loan. Negative amortization can occur when an ARM has a payment cap that results in monthly payments not high enough to cover the interest due. This is NOT good. Your Good Faith Estimate will note if your loan has negative amortization or not. See the Checklist for understanding the GFE, at the end of this chapter.

Note

The note is the legally binding document that details the terms of how the borrower will repay the mortgage loan. This is an important document; you should read it at closing to make sure it is what you were expecting. If not, don't sign it. While the mortgage or deed (depending on the state) is your promise to repay, the note specifies how you will repay. The note should include interest rate, length of repayment, payment due date, details of late fee penalties, when repayment starts and ends, and any other terms on your loan.

Note Rate

As stated in your note, this is the amount of interest you will pay to the lender on an annual basis.

Open-End Mortgage

An open-end mortgage is also referred to as a line of credit. Some home equity liens are open-ended. Open-ended means that you may increase the loan amount per the lender's approval.

PMI (Private Mortgage Insurance)

See the expanded definition in Chapter 16, the Insurance Chapter, and keep in mind that PMI is also a term of your mortgage loan.

Payment Change Date

If you have an adjustable-rate mortgage, the payment change date is when your new interest rate, and therefore new payment amount, becomes effective.

Payment Due Date

The date your payment is due is contractually agreed upon by you and the lender; it is outlined in your note.

Prime Rate

The prime rate, also called the prime lending rate, is the most widely used index for U.S. Commercial Capital Markets. It is used to set home equity lines of credit, ARMs, and, credit card interest rates, just to name a few. The prime rate is influenced primarily by the Federal Funds Rate. This is the rate lenders give their best customers, borrowers that pose the least risk for non-repayment.

Promissory Note

Promissory note is another term for note. It is the legally binding agreement to pay your loan.

Rate Lock

Lock-in is a step that is taken during the loan process to guarantee your interest rate for a certain period of time. The usual time period for locking-in the interest rate is 15, 30, 45, or 60 days. The longer the lock period, the higher the lock fee or the higher the interest rate. This is due to the volatility that increases over time. Per the Real Estate Settlement Procedures Act (RESPA), you must lock your interest rate at least three business days before closing. If your rate is not locked, it is floating with the market and is subject to change weekly, daily, even hourly — just like the price of a stock. Once your rate is locked and you close on your loan within the lock period, the interest rate you locked on is guaranteed for the life of your loan if you have a fixed-rate loan.

Secured Loan

A secured loan is backed, or secured, by real property.

Teaser Rate

This is an introductory interest rate, usually associated with an ARM (Adjustable Rate Mortgage).

Wall Street Journal Prime Rate

This is the most widely used measure of the Prime Rate. The Wall Street Journal surveys the 30 largest banks and uses the number that three quarters of the banks use. When 23 (75%) of the largest banks change their prime rate, the WSJ Prime Rate changes their published Prime Rate as well.

Sample GFE by the U.S. Department of Housing and Urban Development

As provided online at hud.gov/offices/hsg/ramh/res/gfeform.pdf

Checklist: Understanding the Good Faith Estimate (GFE)

IMPORTANT DATES

❏ **The interest rate for this GFE is available through:** For loans that are not locked at the time the GFE is issued there are no restrictions on the amount of time the interest rate must remain available. The interest rate can be available for any period of time. For loans that are locked at the time the GFE is issued, the date must correspond to the locked rate; the lock expiration date.

❏ **This estimate for all other settlement charges is available through:** For loans that are not locked at the time the GFE is issued the estimate must be available for at least 10 business days. For loans that are locked at the time the GFE is issued the date must correspond to the locked rate; the lock expiration date.

❏ **After you lock your interest rate you must go to settlement within ___ days:** For loans that are not locked at the time the GFE is issued you will see N/A. For loans that are locked at the time the GFE is issued the date must correspond to the locked rate; the number of days the lock is in effect (the rate lock period).

❏ **You must lock the interest rate at least ___ days before settlement:** For loans that are not locked at the time the GFE is issued you will see at least a 3 day period, but often 5-10 days. This gives the lender/broker time to lock, re-disclose your loan and get your closing documents prepared.

SUMMARY OF YOUR LOAN

❏ **This section of the GFE is self-explanatory with the exception of the term "initial."** The "initial loan amount" is the amount of the principal loan balance on the date of closing. The "initial interest rate" is the rate that is applicable on the date of closing.

❏ **For the "initial monthly amount owed for principal, interest, and any mortgage insurance,"** this will show one single dollar amount. The amount shown must be the greater of: 1) The required monthly payment for principal and interest for the first regularly scheduled payment, plus any monthly mortgage insurance payment; OR, 2) The accrued interest for the first regularly scheduled payment, plus any monthly mortgage insurance payment. This number does not include the monthly amount for any property tax and/or hazard insurance, whether or not these will be escrow items.

❏ **Prepayment Penalty**—This tells you if there is a fee if you pay off the loan early.

ESCROW ACCOUNT INFORMATION

This lets you know if you have an escrow account and if so, how much your escrow charges will be on a monthly basis.

SUMMARY OF YOUR SETTLEMENT CHARGES

❏ BLOCK A = Your adjusted origination charges

❏ BLOCK B = Your charges for all other settlement services

❏ BLOCK A + BLOCK B = Total estimated settlement charges

YOUR ADJUSTED ORIGINATION CHARGES

❏ **BLOCK 1** - Our origination charge: This is the total of all charges for all loan originators (lenders and brokers). This does not include charges for a specific interest rate chosen, such as temporary buy-down or discount rate. Those fees are in Block 2. If the loan is brokered it will include the Yield Service Release Premium (YSP). If the loan is brokered it will include the broker's fees and the lender fees. Loan originator charges include, but are not limited to: application fee, origination fee, broker fee, processing fee, underwriting fee, commitment fee, lock fee, admin fee, doc prep fee, wire fee, lender inspection fee, loan handling fee, funding fee, re-draw fee, assignment fee, any miscellaneous fees, etc. NOTE: "Our origination charge" cannot change (unless there is an allowable "changed circumstance") and may not increase at settlement. This is for your protection. This number can only go down, not up unless there is an allowable "changed circumstance".

❑ **BLOCK 2** - Your credit or charge (points) for the specific interest rate chosen: This block will show any fees your are being charged for the interest rate chosen or any credits you are receiving from the lender or broker.

YOUR CHARGES FOR ALL OTHER SETTLEMENT SERVICES

❑ **BLOCK 3** - Required services that we select: This block contains the charges for all third-party settlement services (except title services) for which the loan originator requires and selects the provider of the service. Examples of these charges for services generally include, but a not limited to: credit report, flood cert, appraisal, tax service, FHA up-front mortgage insurance premiums (FHA, VA, and conventional if applicable).

❑ **BLOCK 4** - Title services and lender's title insurance: This block contains the charges for the Lender's title commitment/insurance policy premium, along with any fees for title endorsements, examinations, searches, and all charges associated with the title services and settlement agent services. This would include any miscellaneous settlement agent fees such as closing fee, delivery fee, e-mail fee, overnight shipping fee, notary fee, etc. being charged by the title company or closing attorney. Charges that a seller pays as a matter of common practice and experience are not disclosed on the GFE. An example would be the common practice of a locality to charge both the borrower and the seller a separate charge for the settlement/closing fee.

❑ **BLOCK 5** - Owner's title insurance: This is the estimate for an owner's title insurance policy if the borrower is paying for it.

❑ **BLOCK 6** - Required services that you can shop for: This block would be for other services that may be required to complete the settlement transaction. Some examples of these services would be an estoppel fee, survey, pest inspection, structural inspection, well/water and septic inspection, condominium questionnaire, etc.

❑ **BLOCK 7** - These fees are paid to state and local governments to record your loan and title documents.

❑ **BLOCK 8** - These fees are paid to state and local governments to record your mortgage and home sale.

❑ **BLOCK 9** - This is the initial deposit for your escrow account (if you have one). You will know if you have an escrow account from the Escrow account information on page 1 of the GFE. This information in Block 9 will let you know exactly what and how much is included in your escrows.

❑ **BLOCK 10** - This is the charge for daily interest on your loan from the day of settlement until your first mortgage payment is due. For example, if you close on December 31st, you will pay one day of daily interest. If you close on December 15th, you will pay 16 days of daily interest. Mortgages are paid in arrears (opposite of rent). So, if you close in December your January loan payment is due on February 1st. This is where people get the impression that they are "skipping" a mortgage payment.

❑ **BLOCK 11** - This is the amount for the insurance you must buy for your property to protect it from loss. Each policy will be listed as well as the corresponding charge for that policy.

For instructions on the New Loan Estimate and New Closing Disclosure see the Consumer Finance Protection Bureau's website:

files.consumerfinance.gov/f/201312_cfpb_tila-respa_loan-estimate.pdf

files.consumerfinance.gov/f/201312_cfpb_tila-respa_annotated-closing-disclosure.pdf

The Loan Estimate will replace the GFE and the Closing Disclosure will replace the HUD-1 effective with all loan applications taken August 1, 2015 and onward.

(16)

Insurance

There are several types of insurance related to purchasing a home. These insurance products are for your protection and for your lender's protection. Your lender can and will require you to insure your home. Almost all homes bought with a loan require homeowners insurance. If you put less than 20% down on your new home, most likely you will also be required to purchase mortgage insurance, sometimes called private mortgage insurance (PMI). Usually you will not have a choice in your mortgage insurance carrier; your loan type dictates your mortgage insurance coverage and carrier.

However, it is your right to choose your homeowners insurance company; your lender cannot dictate this to you. So, shop around, do your research, and make informed choices. After all, this is the insurance that will protect your wonderful new home in the case of disaster. A home is usually the single biggest item that you will purchase in your lifetime. Make sure you are knowledgeable about how it is protected. Below I will explain all of the insurance types to help you get started in researching and deciding what is best for you.

Remember that mortgage insurance is dictated by your loan type, so, depending on your credit history, certain loan types may end up being much more expensive because of the required mortgage insurance. Ask your lender to explain the differences to you so that you can make a good decision. If your lender does not want to take the time to do this, GET ANOTHER LENDER. The fees, requirements, and guidelines associated with loans can change. I'll explain the why's of that under the mortgage insurance heading below. I'll also explain how mortgage insurance and up-front funding fees affect your APR. Read on!

We suggest that our clients start to shop for their homeowners insurance when they are pre-qualified for the loan and begin looking for a home. There are a few reasons for our suggestion. First, as I mentioned, it is required for your loan, so just like you are looking at different neighborhoods and homes that are right for you, look for insurance that is a good fit. Second, you want to have an idea of how much your insurance will cost, as you are required to have it and must pay it.

Insurance costs affect your monthly mortgage payment. Just as you need to know what your principal and interest payment estimate is before you select your new home, you want to know what the insurance, property taxes, and any CDD or HOA/Condo fees may cost you each month, too. There are also additional types of homeowners insurance that may be required depending on where your home is located or the type of construction. Additionally, there are optional insurance plans that may interest you.

Since all of these costs are part of your new monthly cost of your home, each additional cost affects your debt-to-income ratio and is considered by your lender when your loan is underwritten. If you have estimated incorrectly and your insurance costs are actually higher, this may disqualify you for the loan. That's not something you want to find out at the last minute because you have not done your homework.

More important, YOU want to be comfortable with your entire monthly loan payment since YOU are the one who will be repaying it. Insurance is part of your escrows and is subject to change annually. You may change insurance agencies, but most people don't. You should shop your insurance policy annually for the best coverage. Be sure to ask your licensed homeowners insurance agent lots of questions about what your insurance actually covers and how you are protected. Also ask what your deductible is—how much you will pay first before your insurance kicks in. The deductible varies by insurance carrier and policy, and affects your annual insurance premium (cost).

Different Types of Insurance

Homeowners Insurance
Homeowners insurance is also called property and casualty insurance or hazard insurance. This is to protect your home from hazards such

as fire, vandalism, lightning, falling trees, vehicle crashes, etc. Why can your lender require you to purchase insurance? Well, let's say you buy your new dream home and there's an electrical fire and it burns to the ground. Not good. If you don't have insurance, you're left with nothing but you still owe the lender the mortgage repayment. And, with the home destroyed, there's nothing for the bank to sell to recover the loan if you default on your payments. Make sense? The lender will usually collect one full year of payment of your hazard insurance in advance or at the closing of your loan (on the HUD-1).

Flood Insurance

Flood insurance is required if you are in a flood zone. Actually, according to FEMA (Federal Emergency Management Agency), all of the U.S. has mapped flood zones, but only some require insurance. Other additional flood insurance types are optional, such as Flood Zone X. The way FEMA rates flood zones has to do with the likelihood that your property will encounter a flood every 100 years. High-risk flood zones, such as A or V zones, have a twenty-five percent chance of flooding during a 30 year mortgage. Flood Insurance is most expensive when it's required. If you buy a house in a moderate to high-risk flood zone, currently your lender will require you to secure flood insurance as a condition of your loan. This means that you must secure flood insurance before your loan is allowed to close. Do NOT wait until you get close to your closing date to secure your insurance, as it WILL delay your closing.

Condo Insurance

There's also special insurance required if you buy a condominium. This is called an HO6 or "Walls In" policy. Your master condo insurance is included in your condo fees; it covers the building, common areas, amenities, etc. This means that the condo master insurance protects everything from your unit "walls outside," but not inside your unit. This is why you need the additional policy, to protect everything within your unit walls, such as your appliances, flooring and furniture.

Mortgage Insurance and PMI

Mortgage insurance protects you and the lender in case of default. Default is when you don't pay your mortgage. Mortgage insurance pays the lender if you stop making mortgage payments. Private mortgage insurance, PMI, is for non-government mortgages. For government loans (VA, FHA, USDA) there is a similar insurance product, simply called mortgage insurance (not PMI). In addition to loan default, there are also a few special circumstances that qualify for coverage under mortgage insurance and PMI policies; such coverage may help you to keep your home if you default for a period of time. For example, if you have an FHA loan and you lose your job, you may qualify to have the FHA insurance pay your mortgage for up to one year. If you lose your job and you have a conventional loan, with PMI you may qualify to have your mortgage payments paid for you for up to six months.

The fees for FHA, USDA, and VA mortgage insurance are dictated by the loan type. The U.S. Department of Veterans Affairs insures VA loans. However, thanks to the VA (great VA benefit!), there is no cost to you on an annual or monthly basis. That's great news!

For a USDA loan, there is a nominal fee (paid monthly by you as part of your PITI); in the past there was no annual fee. USDA added this fee in 2012. The insurance cost is 0.30% of your total loan amount. If you had a $300,000 loan amount, that would be $300,000 x 0.03=$900 divided by 12 months in the year=$75 a month for your USDA mortgage insurance. This monthly cost to you should be automatically removed once you have 22% equity or 78% loan-to-value in your home. See the loan-to-value section below.

For an FHA loan, the monthly mortgage insurance varies depending on the down payment. If you put down 3.5% at the time of purchase and your loan amount is less than $625,500, your annual mortgage insurance will be 0.85%. If you put down 5% or more and your loan amount is less than $625,500 at the time of purchase with an FHA loan, your annual MI will be 0.80%. The FHA funding fee stays the same, regardless of your amount of down payment. If your loan amount is greater than $625,500 in parts of the country where that is allowed by FHA, your MI can be as high as 1.05% annually. Here's one of the current negative drawbacks to FHA: the mortgage insurance is now for the life of the loan. What? Yes. Although this was not formerly the case, it is now. So, even if you put down 20% or 50% as a down payment when you purchase your new home, you will still be required to have FHA mortgage insurance for the life of your loan.

Also good to know, VA, USDA, and FHA have upfront funding fees that are dictated by each loan program. A funding fee is simply a fee that the entity charges you to get the loan. For VA loans the funding fee can be waived if the veteran has a 10% or greater disability. The FHA funding fee is currently 1.75%. This can change at any time (not after your loan is closed) as dictated by FHA.

For Conventional loans using private mortgage insurance (PMI), several factors are used to calculate the risk associated with your loan. In my opinion, there are more factors that are used to calculate the cost of PMI for your loan than for your interest rate. There are several major PMI companies that lenders use; some of them offer different protections to you and the lender (for example, how long and will your monthly mortgage payment be covered by insurance if you lose your job).

PMI companies consider whether you will live in the home as your primary residence or if it is a second home or investment property. Your credit score, debt to-income-ratio, loan-to-value (how much of a down payment are you putting down?), where the property is located, and more determine the level of risk and therefore the cost of your PMI.

With conventional loans there is no up-front funding fee, as is the case with government loans. With a conventional loan, the MI should automatically be removed when you have 22% equity or your loan-to-value based on your original loan balance is 78%.

Loan-to-Value
Loan-to-value is your loan amount in relation to the value of your home. This number is a percentage that is calculated by taking your loan amount and dividing it by either your sales price or the appraised value of your home. The lender will take the lower value of the two—sales price or appraised value. For example, if your loan amount is $240,000 and your sales price is $300,000, your loan-to-value is 80%. If your loan amount is $240,000 and your appraised value is $320,000, if your sales price is $300,000 your loan-to-value is still 80%.

Also, MI and funding fees affect your APR. Since these are fees that are added to your loan and monthly payment, they are included in your APR. Government loans that include funding fees and monthly MI will typically have a higher APR than a conventional loan that does not have funding fees.

Government and conventional interest rates can be cyclical in terms of the lowest rate. Currently, as of April, 2015, government interest rates are lower than conventional interest rates. This is based on supply and demand of various mortgage backed securities and other financial factors. As a consumer, it's a good idea to ask your lender to price out several scenarios for you so you can understand the different monthly costs and fees associated with each loan. Here we can do an example of an FHA loan with 5% down payment compared to a conventional loan with 5% down payment. We can show the total costs associated with that type of loan as well as the monthly payment. Right now the government rates are lower, but the MI is higher (depending on credit score), so although the FHA interest rate is lower, the total monthly payment may be higher. In these examples, the total loan payments are within pennies of each other.

Comparing Loan Programs (FHA Loan Example)

FHA Loan with 5% Down Payment, 30-Year Fixed

Purchase Price $300,000.00
Base Loan Amount $285,000.00
Funding Fee of 1.75%... $4,987.50

Total Loan Amount $289,987.50

0.80% Annual Mortgage Insurance Rate ....$289,987.50 x .0080
Annual Amount $2,319.90

Monthly MI .... $2,319.90÷12 months
Monthly MI $193.33

Interest Rate of.. 3.875%
Initial Monthly Principal.. $427.21
Initial Monthly Interest.. $936.42
Monthly MI $193.33

Total Monthly PI & MI.. $1,556.96

Plus property taxes and homeowners insurance

Please keep in mind that any interest rates, loan amounts and payments are examples for illustration purposes only. These interest rates may not be available and/or you may not qualify for this or any interest rate, or for a particular loan type or loan amount.

Comparing Loan Programs
(Conventional Loan Example)

Conventional Loan with 5% Down Payment, 30-Year Fixed

Purchase Price $300,000.00
Base Loan Amount $285,000.00
No Funding Fee... $0.00

Total Loan Amount = ... $285,000.00

0.74% Annual Mortgage
Insurance Rate (varies by multiple factors).............$285,000.00 x .0074
Annual Amount $2,109.00

Monthly MI .... $2,109.00÷12 months
Monthly MI $175.75

Interest Rate of.. 4.125%
Initial Monthly Principal... $401.56
Initial Monthly Interest.. $979.69
Monthly MI $175.75

Total Monthly PI & MI.. $1,557.00

Plus property taxes and homeowners insurance

Remember that currently the MI is never removed from an FHA loan; but, after you have 22% equity in your home with the conventional loan, the MI will automatically be dropped so your payments will be even lower.

Interview with David Miller, Brightway Insurance

David Miller is the Co-founder and Chairman of Brightway Insurance, a national insurance retailer. With 117 locations throughout the U.S. today, Brightway has earned recognition from Entrepreneur Magazine as the No. 1 insurance franchise in the country (2013), from Inc. Magazine as one of the fastest growing privately held companies in the country (2008-2014) and from Franchise Business Review as a "Top

50 Franchise" (2012, 2013). Inc. Magazine also awarded Brightway its Hire Power Award, recognizing the company as one of the top 100 job creators in the U.S. (2012, 2013).

Elysia: We're here at Brightway Insurance and we're going to ask some key questions regarding homeowners insurance today. Would you please introduce yourself?

David Miller: I'm David Miller, I'm the co-founder and Chairman of Brightway of Insurance. We started Brightway Insurance back in 2003, with 1 office and 3 people. Today Brightway has close to 120 offices in 8 states, over 700 associates, and we do just under $400 million in sales each year, up from the $2 million per year when we opened the agency. Now we write well over $2 million in new insurance on a weekly basis. Entrepreneur magazine rated Brightway as the #1 insurance franchise in the country. We have been on the Inc. 5000 for the last 7 consecutive years as one of the fastest growing privately held companies in the country. In 2014, Forbes ranked Brightway as one of the top 10 franchises in the U.S. that you can buy in the widest segment of the $150,000 investment leve—whether it's insurance, food, or any type of franchise. I'm proud of that success, but more importantly very focused on Brightway delivering a different kind of consumer experience. The fact that you're writing a book, trying to focus on the consumer is tremendously important.

Elysia: What are the top 3 reasons people should purchase homeowners insurance (besides lenders require it)?

David Miller: Homeowners insurance is pretty exciting. If you were to turn on the TV, you would think that insurance is all about price. The fact is, there's a lot of really good coverages that protect consumers. For most people, a home is their single biggest asset. Making sure there's a wall of protection that exists around that consumer is what we do in the homeowners insurance business. In addition to insuring the house, every homeowners policy has a number of bundled coverages that are already included; things like insuring any detached structures and personal property, those are covered additionally. Even if you have a claim and have to live somewhere else, your homeowners policy will pay for you to live somewhere else while your home is being repaired.

Perhaps one of the most important coverages, other than insuring your home, that can stand between you and financial ruin is liability coverage. Liability coverage makes sure that if someone slips on your property and breaks their neck (God forbid), and decides to sue you, you have adequate coverage to make sure they don't take everything you have or ever will have. It's interesting, car insurance and home insurance are linked that way. Both insurance types have liability coverage and they protect you against lawsuits. That's one of the things that people don't think about. You see trial attorney ads on the TV a lot these days. Those attorneys are getting money from somewhere—we make sure it doesn't come from you.

One other thing that's important with homeowners insurance is flood insurance. A lot of times people don't realize that flood is not actually covered under a homeowners policy. If your house is in an area that's been developed and has flooded in the last 100 years, your mortgage company will require you to get flood insurance. Most new developments don't have a history; they may be prone to flooding, but may not be in an emergency flood zone. So, you might be put in a position where the mortgage company doesn't require you to get flood insurance. In addition, with climate and changing weather patterns, some areas that didn't get a lot of rain in the past are now getting a lot of rain—we just don't know. It's not only that the ocean's going to come and flood your property, or a river, or a lake, it could even be that the storm drains and systems in your new community may not be able to withstand that sort of thing. So it's something else you should be thinking about when you're buying a homeowners insurance policy.

Elysia: I know that FEMA changed a lot of the maps this year. Has that kept you busy?

David Miller: It has; we try to be pro-active. The government tries to create laws to force consumers to act. We try to do it pro-actively even without regulation. Good agents are having those conversations with their customers every day.

Elysia: Excellent. How did you get into the home insurance industry?

David Miller: I started back in the early 90s. I graduated from college in 1992 and by 1993 I had my first job at Liberty Mutual. I started as a fledgling insurance agent. I worked at that company selling insurance for the first 10-11 years of my career. I excelled and became one of the top three insurance agents in North America for their company. I also had the opportunity to manage a number of their offices in multiple states while I was there, prior to starting what today is Brightway Insurance.

Elysia: That's great. So, along the way, you probably picked up some stories about what your favorite things are in assisting home owners?

David Miller: It's funny—it's not so much the answers you give people, but helping consumers by helping them ask the right questions. Our job as good agents is helping consumers make good decisions. Part of it is, they need to know the right questions to ask, and, you have to ask those questions with them. No one who works in this industry works in a vacuum. Consumers deserve to have a quality loan officer, a quality closing attorney, and, a quality insurance agent that help them through the process and work together. And when it works right, they do have that.

Elysia: I feel so strongly the same way. When people are shopping for interest rate, it's great and banks will compete on rate, they're happy do it, you want the best rate; but, it's so much more important to find the right lender, or the best lender who's going to answer your questions, make sure you understand, and make sure you know all the loan products available to you. Just like an insurance agent would ask those questions to make sure they have the right insurance products.

David Miller: The other piece that's important, too, is making sure the homebuyer understands the different components of their home and what the status is of those components. Using a professional who does inspections of the property is also really important because for folks who have not purchased a home before, this may be a scary part and they may not know how a lot of the different systems work and what they should do. A good property inspector will actually teach you a lot of that while they go through and create that report for you.

Elysia: And, it's an excellent report. The interesting thing is, it's not required for all loan types, but every buyer should really get one. The price you pay for a home inspection versus what you pay for the price of the house makes it a great investment.

David Miller: That's true.

Elysia: What's something that most insurance companies overlook during the application process?

David Miller: Realize there is a period of time the insurance company has to review the application and ultimately confirm or cancel the policy. So, making sure the application is complete and it's accurate is really important. Typically, it's the job of your insurance agent, but making sure you get your agent the right information is so important. Having a good inspection report that has accurate information can be helpful. There are more than 100 different companies out there that are providing homeowners insurance in any given market. Different companies have different appetites—some specialize in older homes, newer homes, homes that are close to the coast, homes further from the coast, homes that are constructed from masonry, homes that get better rates for people with different types of protection devices.

Some companies, depending on the age of some of the issues of the house, will be more lenient or more understanding and some will be very concerned about different hazards: old wiring, older roof, AC systems, windows that haven't been replaced in older homes. It could even be some of the things that maybe you buy with a house that happen to be there, like a trampoline or a pool diving board; all of these things can cause concern. Making sure that the insurance company understands what the risk can be up front, completely, is really the best thing you can do. It's almost like dating. It's far better to not be the person you think the other person wants, but rather the person you are. It's true with homes, too. Accurately saying what it is and what it's not will ultimately get you a very solid answer with the insurance company; that yes they want to insure it, and, yes, this is the final rate. So, those two things, completeness and accuracy, are really important.

Elysia: What do most lenders forget to tell their clients when they are in the process of obtaining homeowners insurance?

David Miller: Well, I think it has to do with not so much the lenders, but the people who work for the lenders who have a varied amount of training. And, again I would say having a lender that cares enough to understand not just what they do, but the other pieces that go along with it. Because at the end of the day, the consumer is buying a home and they are relying on a team of people to help them through the process. The more experienced and more knowledgeable that whole team is about what they do and how that works into that whole process, from the customer's standpoint, the better off they're going to be. That's the most important thing, that your lender is on the same page with the closing attorney and the insurance agent and making sure that everything's done within the timeframe it's supposed to be done, and that there are no surprises at closing.

Elysia: I couldn't have said it better myself, ha ha! Thank you David. I like to say in our industry, we say it's sort of like herding cats. 'Cause everyone is running in a different direction, and if you can make everyone run in the same direction, which is towards the homebuyer's goal line, then it usually works out much, much better for the homebuyer. Finally, is there a place where people can go online to find out more about Brightway Insurance?

David Miller: Absolutely, you can go to Brightway.com. I encourage people to look. What's nice about Brightway is that we're the first real retail insurance agency that is nationally branded through which consumers can truly have it all. Instead of one brand when they go to a retailer, for instance: when they go to State Farm, they get State Farm; they go to Allstate, they get Allstate; when they go to Geico, they get Geico. It's an experience that most people don't like—having to go from one brand, to one brand, to one brand, shopping. More than anything, they feel like they get tired before they get the best price.

What Brightway has tried to do is change that whole experience so that you go to one retail insurance store, where they have local offices in your neighborhood with agents who live in your neighborhood who know you, who can advise you first on the coverages that you need and then, which of the 100 or so companies that write this type of insurance are best for you. That, and having the ability to have all of the convenient buying options is also really important; being able to go online, go to a brick and mortar local office, or, pick up the phone. If you can have it all, most consumers tell us that they prefer to have it all, rather than some piece of it all.

Elysia: In this day and age, everybody wants it all.

David Miller: They do, and we believe consumers, they deserve it.

Elysia: Yes, they do, they do. Thank you for your time David; I appreciate it, and, I feel that you have really given a gift of extremely useful information to our readers.

David Miller: Thank you.

To watch the full interview go to bestmortgagebook.com/DavidMiller

Making Sense of the Jargon

Deductible

Deductible is the set amount of money that you must pay towards the assessed damages before the insurance company pays the balance of the claim. For example, if damages are assessed at $28,000 and you have a $1,000 deductible, you must pay the $1,000 and the insurance company will then pay $27,000.

Inflation Coverage

Inflation coverage is an endorsement to a homeowners policy that automatically adjusts the amount of insurance to compensate for inflationary rises in the home's value. This type of coverage does not adjust for increases in the home's value due to improvements.

Liability Insurance

Liability insurance can be an endorsement to a homeowners policy, or a separate policy, that covers claims that may be due to the owner's negligence.

Mortgage Life and Disability Insurance

This is insurance that will pay off the balance of a mortgage in the case of death, or, cover monthly mortgage payments in the case of disability.

Premium

Premium is the amount paid on a regular schedule to maintain insurance coverage.

(17)

How to Choose a Real Estate Agent

Choosing your real estate agent is just as important as choosing your lender. I cannot say enough positive things about skilled, successful real estate agents. They are worth their weight in gold. A great real estate agent can help your real estate transaction go smoothly, getting you to the goal line on time. A bad real estate agent can cause you frustration, and at worst possibly loss of your down payment. Or, a real estate agent more focused on getting a sale now than taking the time to help you find exactly the home to match your needs and desires may lead you to buy a home in a neighborhood you don't really like, or to buy a condo when a single family home would better suit your needs. Always do your research!

Look for Success & Experience

Choose a successful real estate agent with experience. I think this is important for a several reasons. First, a successful real estate agent has real life experience with buyers and sellers, contracts, neighborhoods and negotiating sales contracts. The more deals the real estate agent does, typically, the higher their level of expertise. This level of expertise should help you with a multitude of things, ranging from negotiation experience, understanding of building types, knowledge of school districts, and reviewing and writing a sales contract with you. They can help you with other things you may not even have considered. Do you want to be near public transportation or have easy freeway access? Do you want the best neighborhood with the easiest airport commute? Do you want your bedroom to face the sunset or the sunrise? A great real estate agent will ask you for answers to questions you haven't yet asked.

Look for a Listener that Hears You

Choose a real estate agent who listens to your needs. After all, it's your new home. Be sure that your real estate agent does a full needs' analysis of what you want: property type, possible locations, budget, and, new or existing construction. They should also be asking you "why?" so that they get a good understanding of what you are looking for and can make suggestions that are a good fit for you. Real estate agents are professionals that can truly be an amazing benefit to you by bringing their knowledge, expertise, and experience to your home search. Indulge in the awesome benefits of detailed conversations with your real estate agent. Your home search is your adventure and your time to enjoy!

Choose Team Sports Over King-of-the-Hill

Choose a real estate agent that works well with others. Remember when we talked about all the players on your team who are working hard to get you to the goal line? All the parties must work together for your success. Make sure your real estate agent is ready to play with your team. A great way to start is to meet with your real estate agent and lender when you are ready to write the offer on your dream home. Everyone needs to be realistic and on the same page with deadlines in the sales contract. It's also a good idea to set up a weekly time for updates. In addition to any additional information requests, we call and email all our clients that have loans-in-process on Tuesday mornings. Everyone knows what to expect and when. This helps everyone feel more comfortable during the loan process.

What's the Difference Between a Real Estate Agent & a Realtor®?

Real estate agents must be licensed professionals to engage in real estate transactions. The laws governing real estate licensing vary by state, but all agents must be licensed by the state where they are acting as buyers' or sellers' agents. Licensed real estate brokers or licensed real estate sales agents may also choose to become a member of the National Association of Realtors®. Real estate professionals that belong to the National Association of Realtors® are bound to a code of professional ethics. The organization handles consumer complaints and investigates possible unethical conduct. Only real estate agents that are a member of the National Association of Realtors® may use the designation of Realtor®.

Is Specialization Relevant to Your Search?

There are quite a few educational certifications a real estate agent can obtain, such as Military Relocation Specialist, Certified Residential Specialist, NAR Green Representative, and, Accredited Buyer's Representative. That's just a small selection of the special designations offered through accreditation and certification through the National Association of Realtors®.

Here is the link to the National Association of Realtors® Certifications: realtor.org/designations-and-certifications

Who's on First?
Buyer's agent or seller's agent? Well, if you're listing your property for sale, you want a seller's agent or an agent who is an experienced seller's agent as well as an experienced buyer's agent. If you are buying a property, you want an experienced buyer's agent or an agent who is experienced with both buying and selling. You want to make sure that your agent has experience and knowledge that will help her/him negotiate the best possible sales contract for you. An agent representing you as a buyer will need to do a needs' analysis that includes what your budget is, what property type you are interested in, where you want to buy, and, how quickly you want to buy.

The agent will send you listings for you to review and then show you homes that you have identified as of interest to you for purchase. Once you have selected the home, the real estate agent works with you to draw up the sales contract and reviews it with you in detail. The real estate agent will also review and write counter offers, if necessary. The real estate agent works with your licensed loan officer to get you to the closing table on time.

Interviews with Gary Keller and Jay Papasan of Keller Williams Realty®

As chairman of the board for Keller Williams Realty®, Gary Keller helps provide strategic direction for the company at large. In addition to his leadership role with the company, Gary and his writing team have penned several national bestsellers: The Millionaire Real Estate Agent, The Millionaire Real Estate Investor, SHIFT: How Top Real Estate Agents Tackle Tough Times and The ONE Thing: The Surprisingly Simple Truth Behind Extraordinary Results.

Jay Papasan, who after a successful publishing career in New York, co-authored the Millionaire Real Estate series with Gary Keller, collaborated on the best seller FLIP, and serves as Keller Williams VP of Publishing.

Elysia: Gary, what are your top three guiding principles for client service?

Gary Keller: Win, win or no deal. Integrity: do the right thing. Customers always come first. When we talk about client service, the definition of a professional is someone who knows what they know and knows what they don't know. When you are faced with a situation with a client and you're not sure of the answer, it's not about looking like a professional, it's about being a professional. Just be honest, and say, "That's a great question. I want to give you the best answer. Would it offend you if I got back to you later today/tomorrow with an answer? I work with an amazing team and I'd love to run my thoughts by them and make sure you're getting the best possible information." Understand your strengths and leveraging the team around you and in your brokerage to give your clients the best service.

Elysia: Jay, what is the key to your success in the real estate field?

Jay Papasan: The key to success is lead generation—time and effort spent generating leads for your business. The agents that focus on this always succeed over others. Because they consistently block time to lead generate, they have more leads. Because they have more leads, they enjoy more opportunity and more choice. When you have enough leads you can afford leverage—people to do the work with you or for you. When you have enough leads, you can be selective about your clients. If a seller isn't motivated, you can afford to be firm on your standards and even turn down the listing. Business that is just outside your geographic area can be referred out.

Agents who don't have enough leads don't view these situations from a position of abundance. They often take business that is marginal or that costs them unnecessary time (which could be better spent finding more business). The successful agents understand this at a deep level and make a firm commitment to grow their business through lead generation.

*Elysia: How do you suggest our readers find the best Realtor®
for their needs?*

Jay Papasan: Through due diligence. Ask people you trust who they recommend. Good agents put their clients first. You want to find an agent that truly listens to you. When you find an agent that listens to you, you will also want to listen back. You will be told exactly what you can expect and what will happen during the home-buying process. This is your opportunity to get very detailed about your mutual expectations—ask how often you'll be in contact, how often you can expect to see homes, and how many properties you might visit in an afternoon. Ask your agent how communications will be handled; by phone, fax, or e-mail, and make sure you share your preferences. Ask if there will be others helping your agent who may be contacting you so that you're not surprised when they do.

Elysia: Please share two pieces of advice you have about mortgages.

Jay Papasan: A mortgage is a serious responsibility and warrants very careful attention to what you can truly afford and what kind of mortgage can best help you reach your financial goals. However, a mortgage is a tremendous privilege. Imagine: if you couldn't borrow the money to buy your home, you'd have to pay cash. If you thought coming up with a down payment was challenging, imagine what it would be like to save the whole purchase price!

In general, you'll probably discover that mortgage loans are less confusing than you might imagine. Actually, what appears as a vast array of loan choices in the mortgage market today are all just simple variations on a few major types.

Elysia: Thank you Jay & Gary, I understand why you have raving fans and a successful growing international real estate company! For more information about Keller Williams go to kw.com and for Jay Papasan and his team check out austinsbesthomesearch.com.

To watch the full interview with Mark Willis, Member of the Keller Williams Board of Directors go to bestmortgagebook.com/MarkWillis.

Realtor® Dolly Lenz on Serving the Client

Dolly Lenz, is a real estate executive with over 25 years of sales, marketing and branding experience. Dolly has become an industry leader having sold over $8.5 billion in properties during her career, a record that has earned her the ultimate "Stratosphere Award", a level of achievement of which she is the sole recipient.

Due to the depth of her experience and the breadth of her knowledge in real estate matters, she is repeatedly sought after to represent some of the most exclusive properties in the world. As a regular guest on CNBC's "Power Lunch", "Kudlow Report" and "Fox News with Neil Cavuto", as well as appearances on MSNBC, Bloomberg TV, and "The View" on ABC, she has developed a broad following and continues to opine on current real estate issues in various media publications including The New York Times, Wall Street Journal, The Financial Times and Barrons. Dolly is a CNBC contributor and is featured on CNBC's documentary series "Mega Homes: Secret Lives of the Super Rich. She is also the host of CNBC's real estate special series "Million Dollar Home" Challenge.

Elysia Stobbe: Dolly, what is your most important guiding principle for client service?

Dolly Lenz: Focus On the Relationship, Not the Transaction. I have always focused on long term relationships with my clients by delivering the best service with the highest of standards possible. I represent their interests first and foremost even if this means potentially advising them to exit a deal if the terms are not favorable to their needs, wants and goals.

I will not sacrifice the confidence and respect of my clients for a single deal. I live that every day in my business. Real Estate Brokers are instinctively transactional in their thinking. This stems from the fact that if the deal does not close, then the real estate agent does not get paid. The natural inclination is then to get that deal closed no matter what. This shortsighted approach may work to close one transaction; however it does not always guarantee the best service for your client.

Elysia: Thank you Dolly, it is easy to see why you have loyal clients!

For more information about Dolly Lenz go to dollylenz.com

(18)

How to Choose a Home Inspector

What is a home inspection? A home inspection is a comprehensive examination of the major systems and components of the home. It is NOT an appraisal. An appraisal uses like comparable properties to estimate the value of the home. It does not examine in detail the systems and components of the home. A home inspector will evaluate the roof, HVAC, plumbing, electrical, foundation, framing, insulation, ventilation, walls, ceilings, floors, step, stairways, railings, garage doors, and, a representative amount of doors and windows.

For a complete list of what to expect and what not to expect your home inspector to examine, check out the ASHI standards of practice and code of ethics at their website: ashi.org

Most loans don't require a home inspection, but I strongly suggest that you have a detailed one done for your own good. Don't you want to know what you're getting into? A home inspection may find that you have a few hundred dollars' worth of repairs or a few thousand. That's something I want to know before I buy a house. You might feel that you are so in love with a home you are prepared to deal with whatever needs to be done. You might be thinking "whatever" could be up to $15,000. What if "whatever" is up to $55,000?

Not all home inspectors are created equal. Some will eyeball the roof from the ground, some will get up on a ladder and walk around to inspect the roof. Some will use infrared technology and camera scopes. Some include a mold screening, a moisture analysis, and, a sinkhole report. Some will charge extra for a WDO (wood destroying organisms) report, wind mitigation letter, and, a 4-point insurance letter. You want to know exactly what you're getting for your money and exactly what reports are included. Do your research and ask lots of questions. Technology has come a long way; make sure your home inspector is up to date with the latest home inspection technology.

Interview with Home Inspector Wally Conway

Prior to presiding over one of the largest home inspection companies in North America, Wally Conway was a Naval Academy graduate and is a retired Navy pilot. With a blend of experiences as a business owner, master marketer, contractor, renovator, investor, TV and radio host, and certified Master Home Inspector, Wally believes, "If you're not having fun doing your thing, you're either doing the wrong thing, or your thing wrong!"

Elysia: What is a home inspection?

Wally Conway: A home inspection will evaluate the physical condition of the structure and systems. It will also identify items in need of repair or replacement. The home inspection will estimate the remaining useful life of the major systems, equipment, structure, and finishes.

Elysia: Why do I need a home inspection if the house was recently appraised?

Wally Conway: Many people confuse the respective roles of the home inspector and the home appraiser. This confusion has caused many people to falsely believe that the home appraiser also inspects the condition of the home. In a broad sense, the appraiser will factor in an obvious deficiency in the condition of the home; it is a factor only in that it affects value.

Elysia: What will a home inspection inform me about that an appraisal won't?

Wally Conway: The home inspection gives you details about the physical condition of the structure and systems. An appraisal does not go into this level of detail and scrutiny. The home inspector should turn on kitchen and bathroom faucets, ovens, HVAC, lights, and open and close windows and doors. The home inspector should check crawl spaces and walk on the roof to inspect these areas. An appraiser is not required to go to this level of scrutiny because they are only evaluating property value.

Elysia: What are the certification and qualification differences between a home inspector and a home appraiser?

Wally Conway: The certifications and education of appraisers and home inspectors are completely different. Most states require that a home inspector be licensed, but a license only ensures that the inspector has the minimum training and education allowable by law.
To ensure that your inspector has the education and experience to deliver the professional peace of mind that you need, you must look beyond the license.

You will want to be sure that the inspector has inspected hundreds or even thousands of homes before "practicing" on your home. You want to be sure that the inspector has recent and frequent experience on homes just like the one that you are purchasing. Ask not just "How many years have you been in business?", but, "How many homes have you inspected total, and how many in the past year?" and, "How many homes have you inspected like my home?" There are numerous independent organizations that certify home inspectors. The most rigorous requirements are those required to earn the designation as a "Certified Master Inspector". Certified Master Inspectors in your area can be found at certifiedmasterinspector.org

---

There are home inspection secrets you need to know.
The #1 Amazon Best Seller Home Inspection
Secrets of a Happy Home Inspector is yours free,
with kindleunlimited on Amazon.

Checklist: Home Inspector Screening Questions

❑ What are your certifications?

❑ Does the home inspector have a certification from one or more of the websites listed on the next page?

❑ Do you have any supplemental licenses, such as the Mold Assessor license?

❑ How many homes have you inspected, 5 or 5,000? (That's a big difference. You don't want to be the home inspector's guinea pig. Just like most anything, repetition is the mother of skill and you want a skilled home inspector looking at your new dream home.)

❑ Do you have a home inspection guarantee? If so, what is it? (One of our local Jacksonville Home Inspector's guarantees is that if they miss anything with a home inspection they will buy back your home. That's a pretty solid guarantee!)

❑ What does Angie's List or the Better Business Bureau say about the home inspector?

❑ What do you find when you Google the home inspector? Lots of good or bad reviews?

❑ Is the inspector licensed in the state and county (if applicable) where your new home is located?

Interview with Home Inspector Mike Munn

Michael J. Munn is the COO and Director of Technical Development at BiltRite. Michael became a Certified Building Contractor in the state of Florida in 1989 after growing up building custom homes with his father. He is a Licensed Home Inspector HI 4086, Licensed Mold Assessor MRSA2238, CIEC, and HUD 203k Consultant A0914.

Elysia: What is a home inspection?

Mike Munn: I liken a home inspection to an annual physical. A home inspection is a comprehensive view of all systems in the home to identify potential defects or items that could become potential defects. Just like a person can look and feel fine—that may not always be the case. Early detection is the key.

Elysia: Why do I need a home inspection if the house was recently appraised?

Mike Munn: Appraisal looks at value, uses cumulative value of components, and assumes they are functioning correctly. The home inspector examines functional condition, evaluates proper function, and, documents defects. Statistically, we find the same percentage of severity of defects in older homes, rehabbed homes, and new construction homes.

Elysia: What will a home inspection inform me about that an appraisal won't?

Mike: The home inspector looks at specific performance of all functional systems (plumbing, electrical, HVAC), structure, building envelope, doors/windows, and overall finishes. We evaluate all of the above through multiple lenses, including life safety, code compliance, best building practices, and energy efficiency, and, we provide information on remaining use-able life span of major systems and appliances. Good inspectors also address preventative maintenance for best long-term performance and durability.

To contact Michael Munn directly and learn more about Bilrite and their services check out their website biltriteqa.com/about.

Elysia: What are the certification and qualification differences between a home inspector and a home appraiser?

Mike: The appraiser background comes from understanding an estimate of value. The home inspector background comes from understanding the technical side of construction and building diagnostics.

Websites

American Society of Home Inspectors
932 Lee St., Ste. 101
Des Plaines, IL 60016
847-759-2820
ashi.com

National Academy of Building Inspection Engineers
P.O. Box 403
Wilkes-Barre, PA 18703
800-294-7729
nabie.org

International Association of Certified Home Inspectors
1750 30th Street
Boulder, CO 80301
nabie.org

National Association of Home Inspectors
4248 Park Glen Rd.
Minneapolis, MN 55416
800-448-3942 or 612-928-4641
nahi.org

(19)

What to Look for in Your Sales Contract

The sales contract is the road map for your purchase. The sales contract is a legally binding document and should be taken very seriously. It includes time deadlines that are critical. The clock starts ticking once your contract is fully executed. Fully executed means that the contract has been signed by all parties. Lack of performance on your part, as well as on the part of your team (your lender, real estate agent, and title company), can put your earnest money deposit in jeopardy. This works both ways. If your seller has obligations, such as repairs to complete, they must perform as well. If not, there are legal ramifications for the seller, as well.

The typical timelines in a sales contract are 5 days for you to make full loan application, 10 days for your appraisal to be completed, 25 days for loan application and 30 days for closing. What if you pick a lender that takes 45 days to close your loan and your sales contract says you must close in 30 days? It may be time to consider a different lender or get an extension for your closing date.

All timelines can be adjusted in your offer to the seller and may be countered by your seller during the negotiation phase before the contract is fully executed. Knowing your loan application, appraisal, loan approval and closing timelines and discussing them with your team is a key component to a smooth, on-time closing.

Additional key components are the home inspection and repairs. The home inspection deadline is usually 10 days. If your sales contract is contingent on the home inspection, then you may back out of the contract if you don't like what you see in the home inspection report. You can also ask the seller to make repairs to certain items in the home inspection report as long as you are within the deadlines in the sales contract.

Key Elements in a Sales Contract

Financing Contingency

This is very important! This allows you to get your binder (earnest money deposit) back if you don't qualify for your loan. Always include this in your sales contract! What if you qualify, but your property doesn't? Without this clause you may lose your earnest money deposit!

Remember, the sales contract is a legally binding document. It's important to read all of the pages and ask questions to make sure that you understand what is expected by all involved parties.

Appraisal Contingency

This is also very important! This allows you to get your binder (earnest money deposit) back if the appraised value does not meet or exceed the sales price in your sales contract. The appraisal will also let you and your lender know if the property is habitable or repairs need to be made before the loan can be approved. Always include this in your sales contract!

The appraisal for a single-family residence is completed on a form 1004. Remember that your loan application is a 1003? Your loan application (form 1003) and the appraisal (form 1004 for a single family residence) are the two most important pieces of information to the lender. The appraisal is the estimated value of your property. That is the collateral that the lender will make their decision to lend or not to lend you money upon.

The appraisal is paid for by you and owned by the lender. You are entitled to a copy of the appraisal and you must sign a document that says you have received it prior to closing. The Appraiser Independence Act of 2010 replaced the 2007 Home Valuation Code of Conduct. One reason that there is strict regulation about appraiser independence is so that the lender has no influence over the appraiser. The appraiser is not directly employed by the lender. Once the appraisers are approved through a strict vetting process, they are selected randomly to perform an appraisal.

The appraisal uses like comparable property sales and makes adjustments up or down to those comparables to come up with a value for the property being appraised. The comparables are adjusted up or down based on square footage, garage, pool, location, fireplace, number of bedrooms, and, floor (with a condo, the higher the floor, the higher the value). Appraisers must be licensed in the state in which the property is located. An appraisal will include information about the neighborhood; for example, if the neighborhood is declining or appreciating in value the appraisal will address this. It will also include a map that shows where the subject property and the comparables used are located with the addresses of each property. Based on the residency and property type, there are a variety of appraisal forms and addendums.

For more details about co-ops, manufactured homes and condominiums, visit the Fannie Mae website: fanniemae.com/singlefamily/appraisers

Title

Title is critical for several reasons. For one, the property must have clear title in order for it to be transferred. That means that the property must be free of encumbrances, such as liens. If you are buying a foreclosure, it may have a clouded title, which needs to be cleared. If you are buying a property that was foreclosed upon, it may take some time for the title to be cleared. For example, there may be more than one bank lien, there may be homeowners association liens, and perhaps a Federal tax lien. The lender or real estate agent will order title work on your behalf from the title company once your sales contract is fully executed. Clear and marketable title is usually due within 5 days of closing. So, the title company must have that information to the lender at least 5 days before your loan is scheduled to close. Without it, the lender is not able to close your loan because there is no proof that the property is able to be transferred.

How you hold title to your new home is also important. If you are part of a married couple you have the choice in some states to choose from "joint tenants" or "tenants in entirety" if it is your primary residence. Title for second homes and investment properties have more flexibility in how the property may be titled. If you are part of a couple that is not married, you can not only choose from "joint tenants" or "tenants in entirety", you can choose who has which percentage of ownership. Some couples choose 50/50, some may choose the percentage based on who contributes a larger portion of the down payment. Its important to discuss the differences of "joint tenants" or "tenants in entirety" with your title company and/or your attorney.

Joint Tenants

"Joint tenants" means that the owners have equal rights to the property. To sell the property, all of the joint tenants must agree to the sale and the proceeds are split equally. Joint tenants includes rights of survivorship which means that if one of the tenants dies, the ownership of that tenant transfers to the surviving tenant(s). In the case of death of one tenant, the property goes directly to the surviving joint tenants due to the right of survivorship, which may bypass the delay and costs of probate. Joint tenants can have up to four owners on the deed and each have an equal share in ownership.

Tenants in Entirety

"Tenants in Entirety" is for married couples and, in a few states, same-sex partners who have registered with the state. The couple owns the property as an undivided whole. If one dies, the property passes directly to the other. In addition, with tenants in entirety, a creditor of one of the individuals may not attach a lien to that property, only a creditor of the couple that owns it. The couple must decide together to sell the property; one of the people in the couple cannot sell it on their own.

Tenants in Common

This does not include the right of survivorship. Each of the tenants may transfer their ownership interest in the property. Tenants in common hold undivided, individual interest in the property.

Survey

All lenders usually require a survey for single-family residences (not co-ops or condos). A survey will show where the structure is located on the property, if there are any out buildings and/or fences and where they are located, as well as any easements on the property. See more about surveys in Chapter 9, Property.

Closing

Closing day is the most exciting part of the loan process! Closing is the day you've been waiting for…and if you have a great team you'll get there. The best team has key players join you at the closing table. This is your lender, real estate agent, and, the closer for the title company.

How it Works & Who's Involved

Closing Basics

Different states have different laws and rules for closing. Some states require that an attorney close your loan, some states require that you close in escrow, and, some states allow for a title company to close your loan. Here are a few of the states that require (not optional) attorneys to close real estate transactions: Alabama, Delaware, Georgia, New York, North Carolina, South Carolina, and, Massachusetts. For specifics on who can close your loan in your state and the benefits of each, ask your lender and real estate agent who they trust and ask them the differences between each, as well as the pros and cons. In addition, ask the title company the differences, pros and cons, in the various ways you can take title to your new home. Also, in some states the document that gives you ownership to the property is called a mortgage and in some states it is called a deed.

The Home Owners Network offers Total Home Support during all phases of home ownership. Great free app, Great discounts and Free emergency hotline. www.homeownersnetwork.com/join-now/

Closing QC

Once your loan is fully approved, it goes through the quality control (QC) process at your lending company. Some lenders do QC simultaneously during the loan underwriting stage, but most lenders do QC after your loan is fully approved by underwriting. Quality control tries to catch anything that the underwriting department may have missed, such as errors in title work; a property that you may be on title with your parents but forgot to mention since you don't make the payment and it slipped your mind; the way your name appears on your sales contract versus your driver's license; your homeowners insurance mortgagee clause and start date; and, whether you are escrowing your homeowners insurance or was it supposed to be paid in full before closing. QC gets to review fun and exciting tidbits like that. Once your loan passes QC, your loan is clear to close.

Closer at the Lending Company

Next, your loan goes to a closer at the lender. The closer prepares your closing documents and instructions for the title company or closing attorney regarding how to prepare your HUD-1 Settlement Statement (soon to be the Closing Disclosure). The closer sends this information to the title company or closing attorney. The title company reviews it, works up a HUD-1 for review, then sends the HUD-1 to the lender. The lender reviews the HUD-1 and approves it or requests changes from the title company. Changes could be as minor as spelling corrections to major items such as seller closing costs assistance. Keep in mind that these types of major changes are surprises you do not want just before closing. But, since there are many entities involved in the loan and closing process, sometimes these things are miscommunicated, or, unfortunately not communicated at all. One more reason why you want a great team that works well together and on your behalf.

Title Company or Closing Attorney

Once the HUD-1 is approved, the lender sends the full package of closing documents that need to be signed to the title company or closing attorney; at this point the lender is able to wire the funds for your loan. The closing documents that need to be signed are usually sent electronically these days, via email as a PDF. The title company or closing attorney prints those documents and the closer from the title company or the closing attorney brings them to your closing. Closing may be at either the selling or buying real estate agent's office, at the title company or closing attorney's office, or, at the lender's office. When the lender wires the funds to the title company's bank account, the title company can see that the wire for closing has come into their bank account, but the title company is not able to access the funds until they receive a funding number from the lender.

Release of Funding for your Home

Most lenders have a list of documents that they need to review in order to release the funding number to the title company. These are documents that are critical to the loan. For example, the HUD-1, deed, ID verification, and note are usually required for funding the loan. Believe it or not, even experienced closers and home-buyers miss dates, initials or may sign improperly. Adding your middle initial if your name does not appear like that on the loan, or, omitting a middle initial if it does appear on your loan may invalidate the documents. So, these nuances can hold up the funding at your closing. Your loan is not closed until it is funded. If these documents are not correct, they must be signed correctly in order to fund your loan. Once your loan is funded, the home is yours. Congratulations! This is the time for house keys, cocktails (or juice smoothies if you prefer) and selfies!

Notify the lender if any of the parties will not be physically present at closing. If you, or your co-borrower (or spouse), or the seller will not be able to be present at closing, let your real estate agent and lender know as soon as possible. A power of attorney will need to be prepared and approved by you, the lender, and the title company—or the closing date must be moved. Also, if your closing is a mail-away, let all parties know. This requires more time since the closing documents will need to be sent a few days ahead of closing day.

And this one time...

Closing Miscommunication Story

A couple of years ago I was working with a borrower that was purchasing a short sale. A short sale is a property that is sold "short" of what is actually due on the mortgage loan of the seller. For example, if you owe $500,000 on the property, but it's only worth $400,000 and you have to relocate, you are "short" $100,000 if you sell the property. The bank may approve your short sale for $400,000 and forgive the difference or make you hold a non-secured note for the *difference. Don't do a short sale if you can help it—it ruins your credit and you usually have to wait another 3-4 years before you are eligible for a mortgage.*

Anyway, back to my story…My clients put in an offer to purchase a short sale property. Their offer was approved, along with the short sale approval letter from the lender of the owner of the property. This approval letter always supersedes the purchase contract. My client had initially asked for $5,000 in seller help for closing costs which was signed by all parties in the sales contract. However, the lender that approved the short sale removed the $5,000 seller help for closing costs and did not include seller help in the approval letter. When the title company received the letter, that additional change was not sent to the lender, not sent to the real estate agent, and, not sent to my client, the buyer. So, we had no idea until the day before closing that our client had to come up with another $5000 to purchase the home.

This is a great example of how my buyer did everything correctly, but the title company that was working on the short sale for the seller dropped the ball and cost my client a nasty last minute surprise to the tune of $5,000. This should in no way reflect on title companies in general, as there are many excellent title companies. However, this should serve as a critical learning point on the importance of a good quality title company.

…at mortgage camp…

Checklist: Closing Documents (Signed at Closing)

❑ HUD-1 Settlement Statement
(Closing Disclosure for loan applications August 1, 2015)

❑ Final loan application aka 1003

❑ Truth in Lending

❑ Good Faith Estimate with intent to proceed

❑ Itemized fee worksheet

- ❑ Risk-based Pricing Notice

- ❑ Notice of Copy to Appraisal

- ❑ 4506T

- ❑ Note, mortgage, or, deed depending on the state where the property is located

- ❑ Itemization of amount financed

- ❑ First payment letter

- ❑ Amortization schedule (initial)

- ❑ Initial escrow account disclosure statement

- ❑ Hazard insurance authorization

- ❑ Requirements and disclosure

- ❑ Hazard insurance endorsement letter

- ❑ Flood hazard determination

- ❑ Signature/name affidavit

- ❑ Borrower's certification and authorization

- ❑ Social security authorization verification form

- ❑ W-9

- ❑ Credit score disclosure

- ❑ Servicing disclosure statement

- ❑ Notice of furnishing negative information form

- ❑ Compliance agreement

- ❑ And, many more if your loan is a government loan.

- ❑ If your loan is a refinance for a primary residence, you will also sign the right of rescission form which gives you 3 days to execute and return if you change your mind and decide you do not want to close on the refinance of your home.

Checklist: Closing Costs (Payments Due at Closing)

❑ Contract sales price

❑ Daily interest on mortgage loan from closing date to end of month

❑ Credit report fee

❑ Tax service fee

❑ Flood certification fee

❑ Homeowners insurance annual payment

❑ Escrows (homeowners insurance and property taxes)

❑ Mortgage insurance premium (if applicable)

❑ Discount charge (if applicable)

❑ Origination fee (if applicable)

❑ Title fees (lender's title policy, owner's title policy, endorsements to the title policies, title search fee, closing or settlement fee)

❑ Government recording and transfer charges (deed, mortgage, city-county-state tax stamps)

❑ Homeowners warranty

❑ WDO/Pest inspection

❑ HOA or condo dues

❑ Survey

❑ Appraisal fee

*These are some of the most common fees and payments. Your sales contract will outline the costs/fees of your purchase.

Sample HUD-1 by the U.S. Department of Housing and Urban Development

As provided online at hud.gov/offices/adm/hudclips/forms/files/1.pdf

The Closing Disclosure will replace the HUD-1 effective with all loan applications taken August 1, 2015.

Government

Government regulation is important to you as a borrower because a lot of the things your lender will ask you for stem from government regulation in the mortgage industry. The requirements related to adhering to standards can be the most disheartening part of the mortgage process. Lenders are now under intense scrutiny not only from the start to finish of the mortgage process, but also after the loan has closed. If the loan defaults (borrower stops paying), the government can audit the loan.

Government institutions also randomly review mortgages after they have closed, as well, to make sure they are compliant. What does this mean to you? More regulations become more paperwork requirements for you, and that also means more questions from your lender. Government involvement is also designed to protect the buyer from unscrupulous lenders. Making sure you actually qualify for the loan you are receiving is key to protecting you. Additionally, regulation is designed to protect you from unreasonable fees.

Each state also has its own regulatory agencies. This applies to banks, insurance, and securities. You want to make sure that whoever you decide to work with is properly registered with the appropriate state agency. It's important to work with a lender who is knowledgeable and understands the in-depth detailed mortgage process, and, is happy to answer your questions at length. As a consumer, you have the right to choose the lender that you think is best for your situation. Assess a lender's knowledge base before beginning a mortgage application.

One way to make a lender assessment is to check out their rating with the Better Business Bureau, either at the BBB website or by telephoning a regional office. Another resource is reviews on

Zillow.com or Trulia.com. On Zillow.com, only past clients of the lender (and real estate agent) are allowed to submit reviews, so the reviews are optional to the homebuyer and cannot be edited by the lender. You can also Google your lender for complaints. We often suggest this to our clients so they can do their own research and form their own opinion.

Sweetened, Condensed History of Government and the Mortgage Industry

The government has been involved with the mortgage industry for a long, long time. In 1934 the Federal Housing Administration was created to foster lending for homes, a response to The Great Depression. More recently, the most visible, highly publicized government action in the mortgage industry was the Federal Housing Finance Regulatory Reform Act of 2008, enacted after the mortgage market crash of 2007/8. Between 1934 and 2008, there were many changes and additions in government action in the mortgage industry. But, since the mortgage meltdown of 2007/8, the government has seriously tightened lending requirements.

And, things continue to change. As of August 2014, would-be borrowers must wait a longer period of time after having a short sale or foreclosure to again qualify for a loan. The change was announced in July of 2014, so any applicants that may have been affected had only one month to apply for a mortgage, or face a longer waiting period for eligibility. If you're on the verge of applying for a mortgage, ask your lender what changes might be on the horizon that may affect your ability to get a loan.

As of January 10th 2014, QM is a major change and meets the requirements of sections 1411, 1412 and 1414 of the Dodd-Frank Act. QM is a new term; it stands for Qualified Mortgage. This was an amendment by the CFPB (Consumer Financial Protection Bureau) to Regulation Z, which implements the Truth In Lending Act (TILA). It protects you, the consumer, by prohibiting the lender from making a higher priced loan without regard to repayment. In easy terms—that means that the lender cannot penalize you as a weak buyer by giving you a higher interest rate without verifying that you have the ability to repay the loan. If you do have weak or risky credit, you may pay a higher interest rate to mitigate the risk, but the lender must diligently verify that you are able to repay the loan at the higher interest rate.

Other changes include the HVCC (Home Valuation Code of Conduct) and Appraisal Independence Requirements. These are both laws designed to enhance the integrity and independence of the appraisal process. This protects you, the buyer, by creating an independent third-party to evaluate your potential home; the lender or real estate agents cannot influence the appraisal report. In 2015 the government continues to develop policy and regulation related to the Great Recession and the 2007/8 mortgage crisis.

Q&A Session

Q: What have government changes done to the mortgage application process?

Elysia: Increased paperwork! Sometimes that means intense scrutiny and intrusion. You may be required to submit paperwork that you had no idea would be involved in the mortgage process. Recently I worked with a client that was required to produce funeral expense receipts, requiring painful conversations with family members. Why on earth would you have to supply such documents? Well, all funds for down payment and closing must be sourced and seasoned. This client fronted the money for his mother's funeral expenses and his family repaid him. So, there were large deposits in his bank account that had to be accounted for in order to use those funds for closing.

Q: How does government involvement help or hurt the buyer?

Elysia: The government involvement means more paperwork for you. Although this is designed to protect you, it's often frustrating. In addition, due to the additional regulation, the banks have had to hire more staff to ensure they are compliant which means, ultimately (according to some reports), more fees to you.

Q: What tips do you have for navigating and understanding government involvement in getting a mortgage?

Elysia: Be sure to ready all of your paperwork, especially your closing costs and appraisal. If you don't know what certain items included in your paperwork mean, ask your lender and/or your real estate agent. Remember this when you are filling out paperwork!

Websites

The short-list of Government agencies involved in the mortgage industry (this title spanning more than one line is your foreshadowing…)

Fannie Mae
fanniemae.com

Freddie Mac
freddiemac.com

U.S. Department of Housing and Urban Development (HUD)
portal.hud.gov

Federal Housing Finance Agency
fhfa.gov

Federal Deposit Insurance Corporation
fdic.gov

Consumer Financial Protection Bureau
consumerfinance.gov

Financial Industry Regulatory Authority
finra.org

Securities and Exchange Commission
sec.gov

Office of the Comptroller of The Treasury
occ.treas.gov

Federal Reserve Board
federalreserve.gov

US Commodity Futures Trading Commission
cftc.gov/index.htm

National Mortgage Licensing System
mortgage.nationwidelicensingsystem.org/Pages/default.aspx

Making Sense of the Jargon

The Fair Housing Act
A law adopted in 1968 and amended in 1988 that prohibits discrimination in all areas of the home buying process on the basis of race, color, national origin, religion, sex, familial status, or disability.

Federal National Mortgage Association (Fannie Mae)
Federal National Mortgage Association (FNMA); Founded in 1838 Fannie Mae is a federally-chartered enterprise owned by private stockholders that purchases residential mortgages and converts them into securities for sale to investors. Fannie Mae was placed into conservatorship of the Federal Housing Finance Agency in 2008. Fannie Mae was publicly traded from 1968 until it was de-listed from the New York Stock Exchange in 2010. Fannie Mae supplies funds that lenders may loan to potential home-buyers by purchasing mortgages.

Federal Emergency Management Agency (FEMA)
The Federal agency that establishes flood insurance rates and terms of coverage, indicates and maps flood-zone areas, directs the activities of the Federal Insurance Administration, issues policies and processes claims. For more information, see fema.gov.

Federal Home Loan Mortgage Corporation (FHLMC or FREDDIE MAC)
A federally-chartered enterprise authorized by Congress in 1970 through the Emergency Home Finance Act to expand the secondary housing market by purchasing residential mortgages insured by the General Housing Administration or guaranteed by the Veterans Administration (VA), as well as conventional home mortgages. It sells participation certificates whose principal and interest is guaranteed by FHLMC. Freddie Mac was placed into conservatorship of the Federal Housing Finance Agency in 2008. Freddie Mac was publicly traded until it was de-listed from the New York Stock Exchange in 2010.

Federal Housing Administration (FHA)
The FHA is a government agency that was created by the National Housing Act of 1934 to advance homeownership opportunities for all Americans. The FHA assists home-buyers by providing mortgage insurance to lenders to cover losses that may occur when a borrower defaults. In 1965 FHA became part of the U.S. Department of Housing and Urban Development (HUD).

Government National Mortgage Association (GNMA)
GNMA is a federal government corporation that was created in 1968 by an amendment to Title III of the National Housing Act. Also known as Ginnie Mae, it is a constituent part of the U.S. Department of Housing and Urban Development (HUD). GNMA guarantees securities backed by mortgages that are insured or guaranteed by other government agencies. GNMA also pools VA-guaranteed and FHA-insured loans to back securities for private investment and is overseen by the U.S. Department of Housing and Urban Development (HUD).

USDA
The United States Department of Agriculture is a federal executive department that oversees and funds USDA loans and performs a host of other functions including providing leadership in agriculture, food, nutrition and natural resources.

HELP (Homebuyer Education Learning Program)
An educational program from the FHA that counsels people about the home buying process; HELP covers topics like budgeting, finding a home, getting a loan, and home maintenance.

Housing Counseling Agency
Provides counseling and assistance to individuals on a variety of issues, including loan default, fair housing, and home buying.

HUD
The U.S. Department of Housing and Urban Development was established in 1965 and works to create a decent home and suitable living environment for all Americans. HUD addressing housing needs, works to improve and develop American communities, and enforces fair housing laws.

Recorder
The public official who keeps records of transactions concerning real property. Sometimes known as a "Registrar of Deeds" or "County Clerk."

Recording
The recording in a registrar's office of an executed legal document. These include deeds, mortgages, satisfaction of a mortgage, or an extension of a mortgage making it a part of the public record.

Regulation Z
Federal Reserve regulation issued under the Truth-in-Lending Act (TILA), which requires that a credit purchaser be advised in writing of all costs connected with the credit portion of the purchase or refinance.

RESPA
Real Estate Settlement Procedures Act of 1974. A law protecting consumers from abuses during the residential real estate purchase and loan process by requiring lenders to disclose all settlement costs, practices, and relationships.

Section of the Act
The section of the National Housing Act that is used in underwriting a particular FHA loan. (For example, Section 203(b) is used for the basic fixed rate loan program for FHA purchases and refinances.)

Settlement Statement
A document required by the Real Estate Settlement Procedures Act (RESPA). It is an itemized statement of services and charges relating to the closing of a property transfer. The buyer has the right to examine the settlement statement one day before the closing. This is called the HUD-1 Settlement Statement.

Stripped MBS (SMBS)
Securities created by "stripping" or separating the principal and interest payments from the underlying pool of mortgages into two classes of securities, with each receiving a different proportion of the principal and interest payments.

Truth-in-Lending (TIL)
A federal law obligating a lender to give full written disclosure of all fees, terms, and conditions associated with the loan initial period and then adjusts to another rate that lasts for the term of the loan.

Truth-In-Lending Act (TILA)
A federal law requiring a disclosure of credit terms using a standard format to facilitate comparison between the lending terms of financial institutions.

Uniform Residential Appraisal Report (URAR)
Standard form used by appraisers to detail facts supporting the value of single-family properties (a.k.a. FNMA Form 1004/FHLMC 65).

Uniform Residential Loan Application (URLA)
Standard form used for mortgage applicants to provide the lender with information essential to loan approval (a.k.a. FNMA Form 1003).

VA (US Department of Veterans Affairs)
A federal agency, which guarantees loans made to veterans; similar to mortgage insurance, a loan guarantee protects lenders against loss that may result from a borrower default.

Special Planning

If getting a mortgage is something you need to work towards because of circumstances of the past, don't fret. You can get a mortgage. You may need to work on all, one, or a combination of some of these things: credit, down payment, and, debt. Realizing the dream of home ownership is possible! With a savings plan and a commitment to establishing or repairing credit, you can qualify for a mortgage in the future. It's within the grasp of most American families; even those who are new to the country may qualify for a mortgage within two years of establishing credit in the U.S. It's the American Dream! Follow the four simple strategies below to improve your credit and reduce your risk to a mortgage lender.

Your Road Map to Home Ownership

Establish a Starting Point

First, establish a financial starting point and set your goal. Identify where you are and where you want to be—then, set your goal. Where you want to be is your goal and you will develop strategies to get to your goal. This is based on what's important to you. How much do you want to save? How much you would like your monthly payment to be (so you can still enjoy all the other things you like to do in life)? How much house do you want to buy? Where do you want to buy? How long should you rent to reach your goals for buying a home? Only you know how much you can save each month. Devise a timeline with a savings plan that is achievable. Always make your goals achievable. You can make it so that you have to stretch to reach your goal; stretching is realistic and doable. The key is to plan and stretch before you buy your dream home, not when you are in it.

Pay Your Bills on Time

This is critical to building good credit. Paying your bills on time counts for as much as 50%-60% of your credit score. The creditors and mortgage banks look at this carefully. If you don't pay your credit cards on time, why would you pay your mortgage on time? You can fix past errors by paying your bills on time starting now. It's a commitment that will lead you to owning your own home.

The timing of bill payment affects getting a mortgage because when you apply for a mortgage, whatever is on your credit factors into your loan qualification. A loan application and your credit history is a snapshot in time. If you just paid off a bunch of debt, it probably won't show on your credit report because the credit bureaus report about one month behind. Remember, your loan application is a snapshot in time, at the time of your application.

If you have paid bills late in the past, that has lowered your credit score because payment history counts for between 10%-20% of your credit score. So, if you have not paid bills on time, and especially if you are not current on all your payments, that will negatively affect your credit score.

If you no longer have bills or debt to pay to show that you can pay on time or you do not have current bills or debt to pay to show that you can pay on time, then you do not have "good" credit because you do not have current active credit to outweigh any bad credit that may be reporting and bringing down your credit score. Current active credit shows that you are now being responsible with your debt by paying your bills on time. Remember, in getting a mortgage you are asking someone to front you the money to buy your home. Think about what you would want to see from a stranger asking you to borrow tens of thousands, or even hundreds of thousands, of dollars. Aim to be the loan candidate you would want to see in the world.

If you have had bad credit in the past, lenders generally like to see 12-24 months of on-time payments. If you have had collections in the past, lenders generally need to see 12-36 months of on-time payments.

Pay Down Your Debt

While you are paying those bills on time, be sure to pay a little extra. Come up with a plan to spend less than you make (a lot less) and pay down those credit card bills. Just because you can get a "free" line of credit, the qualification doesn't mean you should do it. Why have an open line of credit or extra credit card if you aren't sure you can resist temptation?

A good rule of thumb is to attack the line of credit with the highest interest first. So, if you have credit cards with 10%, 15% and 18% interest, you will pay down the balance with the 18% interest first. Be sure to still make the minimum payments for your other monthly obligations, of course— just put more towards the debt that is the most expensive. Then pay off or pay down the 15%, then the 10%. Make sense? Car loans are a bit different since they are usually fixed payments over a period of time. Credit cards are revolving lines of credit that allow you to run up and pay down the balance. Therefore, your balance and payment can change monthly depending on what you charge on a credit card. Car loans, which are installment loans, are different. A car loan has a fixed amount that you were approved for, which is the starting balance, and an installment loan also has a set interest rate with a set payment schedule and set payment amounts (that should not vary unless you pay late). Therefore, paying down the balance on a car loan won't necessarily improve your credit score. Paying a car loan on time for the duration of the loan will help your credit score. Be sure to ask your licensed loan officer what she/he suggests when it comes to your personal credit.

Save Your Money!

A good general rule is to pay yourself first. This can be in a 401K, 403B, TSP, IRA or Roth option. It's best to save before you are taxed. If you have a 401K, you may be able to take advantage of the withdraw option, so you can usually withdraw or take a loan against your 401K without penalty. There are different loan and withdraw options for each type of retirement account. Ask your financial specialist for details. Be sure to consult tax and financial professionals about the specifics, as each person's situation is different. Be sure to ask each financial institution when and under which circumstances and terms you will be able to withdraw funds, so you know where to funnel your savings for your down payment.

When you are working on your budget, a good rule of thumb is to pay yourself 10% first. It's important to pay yourself before your bills. If you can automate this with direct deposit to your savings account it makes it easier; what you don't see you won't spend! Live within your means. How many times have you heard this? It's not rocket science, but it takes discipline. How much to save depends on your budget and your goals. Once you get in the habit of paying yourself first and saving, it's easier to increase the amount of money you want to save for your down payment and other big dreams and goals.

The best way to start is to save it before you see it. So, if your company has a retirement plan such as a 401K or 403B, take advantage of it! This is money you can save pretax! If you are in the military, you may be eligible for the military retirement plan, called a Thrifty Savings Plan or TSP for short. Set aside 10% of your gross pre-tax income to contribute to your future. That's for you. Plus, if you are contributing to a pre-tax account, you don't get taxed on what you save! Get committed to saving. Then you can contribute to a savings or money market account. You should have about 6 months worth of expenses in a savings account for emergencies. If you don't need it, don't buy it. Save your money instead.

If you do not have the option to contribute to a pre-tax retirement plan through your work, it is still important, and still worth it, to set aside money from your paycheck. You may be able to contribute to an IRA or Roth IRA; be sure to do your research. In fact, even if you do contribute to a pre-tax retirement plan, setting aside at least a few more dollars each month can make a major difference in the long run. You will be in charge of your savings plan, so your determination to actively set aside the money is important to your success. Don't self-sabotage, and don't neglect to set aside your savings "just this once." Decide a set amount of money that you can set aside each month. Even 10%-15% is a good start and far better than not saving at all. Choose an amount that will set you up for success.

It can be an amount that you might feel a little pain from—maybe you will feel a little tension from going out to dinner a few less times per month. Will fewer restaurant dinners be a pinch that will feel good because you know it's getting you to your home-ownership dream, or, will fewer restaurant dinners be so difficult to deal with that you will give up on saving? The best strategy is to start with an amount that you can increase rather than decrease. Whether you begin by setting aside $15 or $150 per month, you can build up your savings muscles and increase the weight of your commitment each month.

Another way to set yourself up for success is to know your attainment horizon. When you set your goal—the amounts that you will save, pay down, and pay off—you need to determine how long it will take to reach the goal. Add up the amount you want to save, the amount you want to pay down, and the amount you want to pay off. Next, divide it by 12 to find out how much money per month you must dedicate to reach your goal. If that monthly amount is just not surmountable, divide your goal by a larger number of months until you get to a monthly dollar number that will realistically get you to your goal. Will it be one year, three years, or even five? If you get frustrated after five months, look at your horizon, set your sights, and stay the course.

6 Motivational Ideas for Saving the Dough

1. Think about what motivates you and choose the motivator that will really affect you. Develop a motivational plan and put it into action now.

2. If you use your online or device calendar to set up your schedule for appointments, try using digital calendar alerts on payday to remind you to move money into your savings accounts.

3. Make gratitude a part of your morning ritual. Whatever you normally do each morning, whether sitting with a cup of coffee or taking a run, while doing it make a mental list of 5 things you're grateful for—include being grateful for having the willpower to forgo that unnecessary dinner out so you could put cash in savings!

4. Are you a visual person? Try making a vision board that will motivate you to save money. What will your life look like once you have reached your savings goal? Make a collage and place it somewhere to inspire you each morning. Make sure it's something that gets you SUPER excited—if you're not excited about your dreams, who will be?

5. Check your local library for financial/motivational books. How have other people overcome financial challenges?

6. Set up a rewards plan for savings milestones. What's a free or low cost activity that you don't often allow time for? When you hit a savings milestone, reward yourself with a special day or treat that doesn't tap into your savings.

Questions? Email us at info@bestmortgagebook.com

23

Bonus Tips & Checklists

Elysia Stobbe's Ninja Packing Tips

Pick Up Free Moving Boxes
Okay, so not everyone is going to be cool with used boxes. But, if you are, it will save you some money. You can ask your local grocery store, liquor store, furniture store, or big box store if they have any unused boxes they don't want—and go to town. If they won't give them to you, you can ask if you can buy them at a discount. You can Google stores that sell used boxes. You can also ask friends and co-workers as well. Often you can find used moving boxes on craigslist.

Pretend You Are on Vacation & Pack a Small Bag
When you get to your new home you'll be very happy to know exactly where your PJs, toothbrush, toilet paper, and clean underwear are. You can also throw in a change of clothes for your first day at the new digs, as well as cords/plugs for the favorite electronics you can't live without. I like to add a night light or flashlight to my bag in case I have to use the restroom in the middle of the night. I can be klutzy enough without being in a new place in the dark! Yeah, I should have said get up for water in the middle of the night, but I like to keep it real.

Get Rid of Stuff!
Get rid of whatever you don't need. There's no need to move it to your new home—your nice, clean new home! Donate items in good condition and get that tax write-off. If you haven't used something in a year, think about if you'll realistically use it in the next year. If

---

For more mortgage tips, tools and information
go to bestmortgagebook.blogspot.com

you haven't used something in 5 years, you're probably paying a lot of money to move it around and take up space over the years...let it go to a new home—someone else's new home.

Take Pictures, Pictures, Pictures! (Before & After)

If you are renting and moving into your dream home, take pictures of your old home after the movers have left. This way, you have proof of what your home looks like after you left if the landlord tries to keep your deposit. I had a friend that was diligent in taking pictures when she first moved into her rental and when she left. Needless to say, she got her entire lease deposit returned to her.

Electronics Pictures

Do you remember how long it took you to set up your TV? Hooked up to your game console, movie player, and cable box? Make it easier on yourself and take pictures (yes, more pictures) of your electronic toys before you unplug and pack them. You'll know what goes where and how it connects when you get to your new nirvana. Then, wrap those cords and cables with a rubber band or Velcro strip and label them so you know which of your electronic toys it co-habitates with best.

Use Plastic Baggies as Containers for Small Items

Wrap picture hangers, nails and screws in tape, label what they go to and put them in plastic sandwich bags. Do the same for screws, nuts and bolts in furniture such as TV stands and beds.

Remember Your Essentials!

Its easy to grab a toolbox for your box cutter, scissors, hammer and level (for picture hanging), nails, picture hangers, tape, magic marker, pen, pad of paper, etc. Use a clear heavy weight plastic box for trash bags, power strips, extra toilet paper, paper towels, cleaning supplies. Also, pack and label one of your kitchen boxes with the items you'll want to use in the first few days like your coffee maker, sugar, juicer, essential spices, favorite pot and pan.

Pack Your Boxes by the Room

This makes it easier to know what's what and where it goes. Labeling the boxes correctly is key. Don't mix boxes or you'll be frustrated beyond belief when you are unpacking or even worse not finished unpacking and you need something and can't find it. Been there, done that!

Use Clothing and Bath Towels to Wrap Breakables

Why waste money on bubble wrap when you've got clothes and towels to pack? You can kill two birds with one stone so to speak. Use those bath towels, t-shirts, sweatshirts & socks to pack your fragile treasures. You can put bed sheets around picture frames, glasses in socks and wrap t-shirts around plates. Blankets come in handy for packing delicate goodies as well. Just remember to use common sense when packing your breakables.

Leave Your Clothing in Drawers

Don't make this harder than it has to be. Just think, a bureau or dresser drawer is a box with no top, right? So why create more work by removing your clothes and packing them. Just leave your shorts, pants, t-shirts and underwear in the drawers. Remove the drawers from the dresser and wrap them with shrink wrap or clingy plastic wrap (lots of wrap!) so nothing falls out. Remember you can use your soft clothing to pack breakables and put them in the drawer too.

Pack Boxes the Opposite of What Will Fit. What?

Pack small lightweight objects in big boxes and larger heavy items in small boxes. Why? Your movers will love you. If you don't have movers, your friends helping you move will love you even more (especially after you buy them beer and pizza!). Also, packing this way helps ensure that your goods don't bust out of the bottom of the box. If you have a box with mixed items both heavy and light, just act like you're at the grocery store; heavy items on the bottom, lighter items on top. Don't crush your bread with a can of soup!

Hanging Clothes

Why would you take them off the hanger? Just leave them on so that when you get to your new place all you have to do is put them back up in your closet. This is where I will break down and spend some money for a wardrobe box if necessary. That's money well spent.

Clean Up Your Mess Before You Go

You would be amazed how a magic eraser will remove marks from your walls. For nail holes, use putty or soap to fill holes in white walls. Soap comes in a variety of colors if you want to give it a try on your colored walls. Either way, you'll be clean.

Do You Have Any Area Rugs?

Don't move those dirty rugs to your new slice of heaven! Now's a great time to have them cleaned! If you are moving locally drop them off at the dry cleaners a day or two before you move and pick them up after you have moved in for a fresh perspective. If you are moving inter-state, be sure to allow time for the dry cleaners to clean them before your movers (or your friends) come with the moving truck. Your rugs will return clean, rolled in paper or plastic wrap, and ready to move.

Checklist: Comparing Homes

Let the Games Begin!

On the next page, you'll find a sample home comparison checklist. You can use such a checklist to carry with you when viewing homes. It's a great reminder checklist to make sure you inspect what's important to you—sometimes it's easy to get lost in the excitement of touring a home. After our example checklist, we've provided a blank list for you to use to clarify the must-haves and the would-be-nice features of your ideal home.

Don't forget to factor in your FUTURE NEEDS! What will you need in 3 years, or 5? Think about your future needs as well as your immediate needs. Buying a home now that's big enough to accommodate a growing family (future children or in-laws) or a home-based business may be a smarter financial move than having to find a bigger place in just a few years.

If you're looking at newer construction homes, you may want to include certain features that you would like to see in a modern home, such as bamboo flooring or quartz countertops. If historic homes fill your heart, you might want to include checklist items that won't empty your wallet later, such as updated windows, new HVAC system, or up-to-code electrical wiring and circuit breakers.

Checklist: Comparing Homes

Sample list of comparision considerations for house hunting

Features	Property 1	Property 2	Property 3
Easy commute			
Outside open balcony or patio			
Master bedroom (12x14 plus)			
Master bathroom			
2 bed plus den			
2 parking spaces			
Laundry room			
Dishwasher			
Allows for future rentals			
Near a park			
Big windows			
High ceilings			
Whirlpool tub			
Radiant heated floors			
Home office/study			
Ceiling fans			
Hardwood floors			
List Price:			
Offer Price:			

Checklist: Comparing Homes

Sample list of comparision considerations for house hunting

Features	Property 1	Property 2	Property 3
Fireplace			
Landscaping			
Pool			
List Price:			
Offer Price:			

Thank you for taking the time to read my book. I hope you have found the information useful in your quest for a residential mortgage as well as during your home buying process.

If my team and I can be of service to you please let us know at info@bestmortgagebook.com. It is through our service to you, our clients, that we are able to help fulfill the dream of home ownership across the country.

Thank you for dreaming!

To check out my blog, go to:
bestmortgagebook.blogspot.com

To subscribe to my home buyer video tips, go to:
youtube.com/watch?v=YsL6BuJ8b-M

For sponsorship opportunities, go to:
sponsorbestmortgagebook.info

Made in the USA
San Bernardino, CA
19 August 2018